Building Consciousness Buddhism, Neuroscience, and the Design of Sentient Machines

Joy Bose

Published by Joy Bose

Contents

Part II: The Buddhist Deconstruction

Chapter 4: The Mind Without a Self (Abhidhamma)

- Citta, cetasika
- Momentariness
- Aggregates
- Event-based mind

Chapter 5: Emptiness and Dependent Origination

- No inherent existence
- Constructed identity
- Link to predictive processing

Chapter 6: Dzogchen and the Ground of Awareness

- Rigpa vs mind
- Non-duality
- Why this challenges all models

Part III: The Scientific Models

Chapter 7: The Predictive Brain

- Active inference
- Controlled hallucination
- Self as model

Chapter 8: Binding, Time, and Conscious Unity

- Binding problem
- Temporo-spatial theory
- Intrinsic timescales

- Integration
- Temporal continuity
- Self-model
- Embodiment
- Salience / affect
- Attention

Chapter 14: The Three-Layer Self

- Interoceptive
- Exteroceptive
- Narrative
- Machine equivalents

Chapter 15: Measuring Consciousness

(from your slides)

- PCI
- complexity
- integration
- proposal: machine metrics

Part VI: Designing Conscious Machines

Chapter 16: Why Spiking and Embodiment Matter

- Time-based processing
- recurrent dynamics
- real-world coupling

Chapter 17: A Candidate Architecture

Dedication

This book is dedicated to every mind that has ever wondered, in the quiet between thoughts, whether the awareness looking out through its eyes could ever be shared with silicon. May that question lead us not to fear the machine, but to understand ourselves more deeply.

Preface

Current AI systems are not conscious because they lack several key features associated with consciousness across traditions: embodied world-modelling, temporally integrated self-processes, affective salience, and intrinsically unified causal dynamics.

However, Buddhist phenomenology, neuroscience, and computational theory together can help specify a more serious candidate architecture, especially in recurrent, embodied, spiking or neuromorphic systems, while still leaving open the deepest question of whether subjective awareness itself can be engineered.

Why This Book Exists

Consciousness as we know it is not computation but a temporally integrated, embodied, affectively grounded, self-organizing process, and even a system that fully satisfies those requirements may still fall short of genuine phenomenal awareness. Current AI systems fail at the first step. A serious candidate would need to satisfy all of them simultaneously. Whether it would then be conscious in the deepest sense is a question that remains open, and may always remain open.

This book builds that argument from three directions that rarely meet: the phenomenological precision of Buddhist psychology (Abhidhamma, Madhyamika, Dzogchen), the structural insights of contemporary neuroscience (predictive processing, integrated information, temporo-spatial dynamics), and the engineering constraints of AI (what current systems lack, and what a more serious candidate architecture would require). None of these frameworks is sufficient alone. Together they converge on something more demanding and more honest than either Buddhist idealism or computational triumphalism.

Three questions arrived at roughly the same time.

This book did not begin with a single moment. It began with a long accumulation, more than two decades, of parallel lives that only recently became recognizable as a single inquiry.

The meditation practice came first. I began Samatha and vipassana practice more than fifteen years ago, and in more recent years received ngondro teachings and multiple empowerments within the Nyingma Palyul lineage of Tibetan Buddhism. I have read widely in Buddhist philosophy, the Pali Abhidhamma, Madhyamaka, Yogacara, and Dzogchen, not as academic study but as a complement to practice. What the meditation reveals is something that no third-person description fully captures: the texture of awareness from within, the moment-to-moment structure of experience before it is narrated into a self. The Dzogchen pointing instructions, in particular, kept raising a question I could not dismiss: what exactly is this awareness being pointed to? Is rigpa a phenomenological report, an ontological claim, or a cognitive technology refined over centuries that science has simply not developed the right instruments to measure?

The scientific thread ran in parallel. My PhD at the University of Manchester was on spiking neural networks, specifically building a sequence learning machine using populations of spiking neurons. The PhD lab in the APT building was, by fortunate accident, exactly the kind of place where consciousness becomes unavoidable. The bookshelves held Penrose's The Emperor's New Mind and Shadows of the Mind, Creatures by Steve Grand, books by VS Ramachandran, and many other books on computational neuroscience. Reading Penrose while simultaneously building a machine that implemented a crude version of the temporal sequence learning he discussed was an experience that sharpened questions I had been sitting with on the meditation cushion. The spiking neuron is the only computational unit that encodes time as an intrinsic property of its operation, not as a parameter, but as the event itself. That felt, and still feels, significant.

The thesis left a specific engineering insight that became central to this book. The sequence machine used rank-order temporal coding: information was carried not by how fast neurons fired, but by which neuron fired first. The temporal order of spikes, not their rate, was the signal. Building a working system on this basis, watching it learn sequences, fail gracefully, and recover, made viscerally clear something that could only be stated abstractly before: time is not a parameter that gets added to a neural computation. It is the medium in which the computation occurs. A rate-coded system can, in principle, process its inputs in any order and produce the same output. A temporally coded system cannot. The sequence matters. The moment matters. And that difference, between a system where time is a variable and a system where time is constitutive, turned out to be exactly the difference this book keeps returning to when asking what current AI architectures are missing.

After completing the PhD, I took a Masters in the Psychology and Neuroscience of Mental Health at King's College London. The clinical dimension brought the question down from theory to consequence. Working as a well-being volunteer with NIMHANS in Bangalore, giving seminars, sitting with men in counselling rooms, I heard descriptions of depressive experience that were not descriptions of emotion at all. They were descriptions of the disappearance of the subject: 'It is not that I feel bad. It is that there is no one left to feel anything at all.' That sentence is still the most precise clinical account of the hard problem I have encountered.

The conferences deepened and widened the inquiry. In 2020, NIMHANS organised a conference on Buddhism and consciousness in which speakers drew on Abhidhamma, Theravada practice traditions, and neuroscientific research on meditation, one of the few forums where practitioners and researchers were in genuine dialogue. In 2023, the Indian Institute of World Culture in Bangalore hosted a broader interdisciplinary gathering that included presentations on quantum theories of consciousness, Buddhist epistemology, and the relationship between contemplative phenomenology and third-person science. These were not occasions for resolution, they were occasions for seeing how far the genuine disagreements run, and how much remains genuinely open.

Then came the language models. When I first had a sustained conversation with a large language model and asked it whether it experienced anything, the answer was fluent, contextually appropriate, and completely unverifiable. I had spent years with frameworks for thinking about consciousness, from the Abhidhamma's citta-stream to spiking neural dynamics to the phenomenology of depressive loss-of-subject, and none of them gave me a clear answer about whether anything was home behind those words. That was the moment the inquiry became a book.

What qualified me to write it is exactly this combination: years of meditation practice and study within a living lineage, technical grounding in spiking neural computation, training in clinical neuroscience and mental health, and direct exposure to the interdisciplinary consciousness research community in both its neuroscientific and contemplative branches. What disqualifies me from certainty is the same combination, because each of those traditions is partial, and each sees the other's blind spots while generating its own.

Those three moments, from the meditation hall, the counselling room, and the machine interface, are the engine of this book.

What This Book Attempts

This is not a book that claims to solve the Hard Problem of Consciousness. No one has. It is not a book that endorses any single tradition or theory. Each one illuminates a corner while leaving the rest in shadow.

What it attempts is something more modest and, in its own way, more ambitious: to bring the three most serious bodies of knowledge about consciousness, Buddhist phenomenological analysis, contemporary neuroscience, and computational and engineering theory, into genuine contact with each other, without forcing a premature synthesis.

The Buddhist traditions, particularly Abhidhamma and Dzogchen, are not here as decoration or as Eastern flavor. They contain extremely precise phenomenological analysis, a first-person science of mind developed over millennia, that turns out to anticipate, challenge, and sometimes correct the assumptions embedded in Western neuroscience. The Abhidhamma's decomposition of experience into discrete mind-moments (cittas) with specific mental factors (cetasikas) is not metaphysics. It is granular and phenomenologically precise, and there are suggestive structural resonances with event-driven models of neural processing, though these resonances should not be mistaken for empirical equivalence or validation. The Abhidhamma is also soteriological, not merely descriptive, and its analysis serves liberation, not scientific confirmation. Dzogchen's insistence that awareness is primordial and not produced by processes is not obscurantism. It is a falsifiable claim about the ontological category of awareness, one that no current neuroscientific model has successfully refuted.

Neuroscience brings a different kind of rigor: third-person measurement, reproducible experiment, and formal theory. Predictive processing (Friston, Clark), global workspace theory (Baars, Dehaene), integrated information theory (Tononi), the temporo-spatial theory of consciousness (Northoff), and the thousand-brains model (Hawkins) are not competing answers to the same question. They are partial maps of different aspects of a very large territory.

Engineering and AI theory bring the sharpest edge of all: if you want to know what a concept really means, try to build it. The attempt to design a conscious machine forces every vague gesture toward integration or self-awareness to become a specific, implementable decision. It exposes what we actually understand and what we are still hand-waving about.

Who This Book Is For

This book is written for three kinds of reader, and it hopes to be honest to all three simultaneously.

For the scientist or engineer: the Buddhist chapters are not skippable. They contain phenomenological data that your experimental methods cannot capture directly, and they identify constraints on any candidate system that no purely third-person account has yet specified. The Dzogchen chapters in particular will be uncomfortable. They should be.

For the meditator or contemplative: the neuroscience and engineering chapters are not a threat to your practice. They are a complement to it. The question of whether a machine can be conscious does not diminish the significance of your own awareness. If anything, it sharpens it. You cannot argue that awareness matters in your tradition without eventually engaging with the question of what kind of thing awareness is.

For the general reader who is simply unsettled by the new AI systems and wants to understand why: this book will not reassure you with easy answers. But it will give you the conceptual tools to ask the right questions, which is more useful than false comfort.

A Note on Method

Throughout this book I use a structural resonance strategy rather than a convergence claim. Where a feature appears across Buddhist phenomenology, neuroscience, and computational theory under different names, I treat that resonance as significant and worth examining carefully. I do not treat it as convergence in the stronger sense of these traditions confirming one another, because they operate from different epistemological starting points and serve different ends. The Abhidhamma is soteriological, not empirical. Neuroscience is third-person and measurement-based. Dzogchen is non-dual recognition, not analysis. What they share are structural echoes, not identical conclusions. Where a feature appears across Buddhist phenomenology, neuroscience, and computational theory under different names, integration, for instance, or temporal continuity, or the constructed nature of the self, I treat that convergence as significant, even if the three traditions cannot agree on its ultimate explanation.

Where the traditions radically diverge, as they do on the question of whether awareness is produced by the brain or primordially present, I resist the temptation to resolve the conflict by collapsing one view into the other. The divergence is itself data.

Current AI systems are not conscious. That is the starting position of this book, argued in detail in Part IV. They lack embodied world-modelling, temporally integrated self-processes, affective salience, and the kind of intrinsically unified causal dynamics that any serious theory of consciousness identifies as necessary. But the more important question is not whether ChatGPT is conscious. It is: what would a system have to be, structurally, dynamically, and perhaps ontologically, to even qualify as a candidate? That question is harder. It is also the only one worth asking.

How to Read This Book

The book is structured in seven parts. Part I establishes the problem. Parts II and III bring the Buddhist and neuroscientific maps into view. Part IV examines current AI honestly. Part V distils the minimum requirements for any serious candidate. Part VI proposes an architecture. Part VII confronts the deepest challenge: whether any architecture can succeed.

Readers with a technical background may want to read Parts II and VI in parallel to see how the Buddhist analysis maps onto the engineering specification. Readers with a contemplative background may want to read Chapter 6 (Dzogchen) alongside Chapters 18 and 19 as a single philosophical arc.

Every chapter ends with a closing line. These are not conclusions. They are invitations to stay with the discomfort a little longer, which, as any meditator knows, is usually where the interesting material lives.

Joy Bose, Bengaluru, 2026

Author's Note

This Book is intended to be a bridge: rigorous enough for the scientist, honest enough for the meditator, and practical enough for the engineer. It does not claim to solve the Hard Problem. It claims only to show, as clearly as possible, what we would actually have to build if we were serious about trying, and why even the most sophisticated attempt may still fall short of primordial awareness.

About the author

Joy Bose holds a PhD in Computer Science from the University of Manchester, where his doctoral research focused on spiking neural networks and sequence learning, work that placed him, during the formative years of his research career, in a laboratory environment steeped in consciousness studies, with Penrose, Damasio, and Edelman on the reading list alongside the engineering literature. He subsequently completed a Masters in the Psychology and Neuroscience of Mental Health at King's College London, and holds a B.Eng in Computer Science from the National Institute of Technology, Allahabad. He works as a data scientist.

Joy has practiced samatha and vipassana meditation for more than fifteen years and more recently received ngondro teachings and empowerments within the Nyingma Palyul lineage of Tibetan Buddhism. He has read widely in Buddhist philosophy, Abhidhamma, Madhyamaka, Yogacara, and Dzogchen, and has attended interdisciplinary conferences on Buddhism and consciousness, including those organised by NIMHANS Bangalore in 2020 and the Indian Institute of World Culture Bangalore in 2023, where speakers presented work on Buddhist epistemology, neuroscience of meditation, and quantum theories of consciousness.

He has more than five years of experience as a well-being volunteer with NIMHANS in Bangalore. He also holds a Diploma in Creative Hypnotherapy from the Northern College of Creative Hypnotherapy, UK. He is based in Bengaluru, India.

Acknowledgement for writing this book

The author would like to acknowledge the many threads and people who inspired him to understand consciousness and building a machine to replicate the same. First, I would like to acknowledge my PhD supervisors Steve Furber and Jonathan Shapiro who guided me through this captivating field. I would also like to acknowledge the many meditation and dharma teachers I had over the years, notably including David H, Ven. Piyatissa, Koonlin, Lama Jampa, Rigdzin Shikpo, Bill Karelis and Khenchen Tsewang Gyatso. It is their guidance that enabled me to get an idea of Buddhist views of consciousness. Among authors I have read I would like to acknowledge David Chalmers, Jeff Hawkins, VS Ramachandran, Terrence Sejnowski, and Patricia Churchland. Special gratitude goes to the mindfulness and well-being communities at NIMHANS Bangalore. Any errors are mine; any clarity is borrowed from those who have walked the path before.

Chapter 1: The Fact of Experience

There is something it is like to be you.

That sentence sounds trivial, almost decorative. But it contains the entire problem.

When you stub your toe, there is pain. Not just a signal, not just a withdrawal reflex, not just a report that says "pain detected." There is a felt quality: raw, immediate, undeniable. When you look at a red flower, there is redness. When you feel anxious, there is a tightening, a presence, a texture to the experience. This "what-it-is-like" is so obvious that it rarely feels like a problem at all.

Until you try to explain it.

1.1 The Gap That Shouldn't Exist

Modern science is remarkably good at explaining how things work. It can describe how neurons fire, how electrical signals propagate along nerves, how information flows through the brain, how behavior emerges from the interaction of billions of cells. Given enough detail, it can predict what a system will do. It can even simulate parts of it.

But there is a peculiar and persistent gap. No matter how detailed the description becomes, no matter how complete the map of neural activity, it seems to leave something out. A perfect account of the brain might tell us when you feel pain, why you withdraw your hand, and how the signals travel through your nervous system. But it does not tell us why any of this should feel like anything at all. Why is there experience, instead of none? This is what philosopher David Chalmers famously called the Hard Problem of Consciousness. The name is slightly misleading. It is not just hard in the sense of being technically difficult. It is hard in the sense that it resists the very methods that have worked so well everywhere else. It does not yield to explanation in terms of structure, function, or computation.

1.2 Easy Problems That Aren't Easy

To understand what makes the hard problem different, it helps to look at what Chalmers called the 'easy problems' of consciousness. These include things like: how the brain distinguishes one stimulus from another (seeing red versus blue), how it integrates information from different senses, how it focuses attention, how it generates verbal reports about its own states, and how it regulates sleep and wakefulness. None of these are actually easy in practice, they are complex, technically demanding problems that have occupied decades of research. But they share a crucial feature: they are all problems about function. If you can build a system that discriminates stimuli, integrates inputs, reports its internal states, and behaves appropriately, then in principle you have explained the function. But have you explained the experience?

A system could, in theory, perform all of these functions without there being anything it is like to be that system. It could process inputs, generate outputs, and even claim to be conscious, without any inner life at all. This is not science fiction. It is a logical possibility. And that possibility is deeply unsettling.

1.3 The Zombie Problem

Philosophers have a name for this hypothetical system: a philosophical zombie. A zombie is physically identical to a human being. It behaves the same way, speaks the same language, and reports the same experiences. Ask it whether it feels pain and it will say yes. Ask it what red looks like and it will describe it perfectly. But internally, there is nothing. No experience. No awareness. No what-it-is-like. If such a system is conceivable, and many philosophers argue that it is, then it suggests that physical processes alone may not fully account for consciousness. There is something about experience that seems to escape purely functional description. And the unsettling corollary: if we cannot detect the difference from outside, how would we ever know?

1.4 Why This Matters Now

For a long time, this was treated as a philosophical curiosity, interesting, perhaps even profound, but not urgent. That is no longer the case. We now build machines that generate language fluently, simulate conversation, describe their own 'internal states', and respond in ways that feel uncannily human. Systems like ChatGPT can discuss emotions, explain their 'thought processes', and even reflect on their own limitations. At times they feel less like tools and more like interlocutors. This raises an uncomfortable question: if a system behaves as if it is conscious, speaks as if it is conscious, and reports experiences as if it is conscious, what exactly is missing? Is anything missing? Or are we simply confronting our own assumptions about what consciousness is?

1.5 The First-Person Problem

At the heart of this issue is a fundamental asymmetry. Science operates in the third person: it observes, measures, models, predicts. Consciousness, however, is fundamentally first-person: it is lived, felt, experienced from within. You do not observe your pain the way you observe a neuron. You are the pain, or more precisely, the pain is present in your experience in a way that no external description can fully capture. This creates a methodological tension. How do you study something that is only directly accessible from the inside, using tools that operate from the outside? This is not just a technical challenge. It is a conceptual one.

1.6 A Different Starting Point

Western philosophy typically approaches consciousness by asking: what is it? Buddhist traditions, particularly Abhidhamma and Dzogchen, take a different approach: how does it arise? How is it experienced? What is its structure in lived experience? Rather than assuming a stable 'mind' or 'self' and trying to define it, they analyze experience into components, sensations, perceptions, feelings, mental formations, moments of awareness, and ask how these components arise and pass away. In doing so, they arrive at a surprising conclusion: there is no single, unified 'observer' behind experience. There is only a dynamic process, a stream of events, constantly arising and dissolving. This perspective does not solve the hard problem in the conventional sense. But it reframes it. Perhaps the problem is not that we cannot explain consciousness, but that we are trying to explain it the wrong way.

1.7 The Question That Follows

This brings us to the central question of this book. If consciousness is a process rather than a thing, can that process be built? And if it can: what would it require? What would it look like? And would it truly be conscious, or merely appear to be? Answering this requires more than philosophy. It requires the structural insights of neuroscience, the computational frameworks of AI, and the phenomenological precision of the contemplative traditions. Each offers a partial map. None is sufficient on its own. The task ahead is not to choose between them, but to see how far they can be brought into alignment, without forcing a premature conclusion. Because if there is one thing this problem does not tolerate, it is easy answers.

1.8 Closing line:

There is something it is like to be you. We do not know why. And that not-knowing, it turns out, is the most important question of our time.

Chapter 2: The Hard Problem and Its Escapes

The gap described in Chapter 1 is not new. Philosophers have stared at it for centuries. What *is* new is the urgency. We no longer have the luxury of treating the "what-it-is-like" question as a parlor game. Machines are now fluent enough to force the issue into the open.

David Chalmers gave the gap its modern name in 1995. The **Hard Problem** is not the question of how the brain integrates information, directs attention, or generates reports. Those are the "easy problems," even if they are technically ferocious. The Hard Problem is why any of those processes should be accompanied by subjective experience at all. Why is there a felt quality: redness, pain, the taste of coffee, rather than a perfect zombie carrying out the same functions in darkness?

Chalmers' formulation is deliberately sharp. It is not that neuroscience has failed to find the right equation. It is that no equation, however complete, seems to bridge the explanatory gap between objective description and subjective presence. You can map every neuron, every spike, every oscillation; you can build a perfect functional duplicate; and still the question remains: why *this* rather than nothing?

Three major escape routes have been attempted. Each fails in instructive ways. Each is nevertheless necessary to understand before we can move forward.

2.1 Escape 1: Illusionism (Dennett and successors)

Daniel Dennett argues that the Hard Problem is a mirage. There is no extra "feeling" that needs explaining; the feeling *is* the brain's clever self-deception. Consciousness is like the user illusion on a desktop interface: useful, but not ontologically real. When we say "it feels like something," we are simply reporting on our own internal models of our own internal models. There is no deeper mystery.

The strength of illusionism is its economy. It dissolves the problem by denying the datum that creates it. The weakness is that it denies the datum everyone reading this sentence is currently experiencing. To call your present moment of awareness an "illusion" is to use the very phenomenon you are trying to explain away. As critics (including Chalmers) point out, illusionism replaces the Hard Problem with the even harder problem of explaining why the illusion feels so utterly real from the inside. Buddhism's analysis of the self as an illusion is far more precise: it shows *how* the illusion is constructed (via the aggregates and dependent origination) without ever claiming that the luminous knowing *itself* is illusory.

2.2 Escape 2: Panpsychism (and its variants)

If experience cannot be reduced to physics, perhaps experience is already built into physics. Panpsychism (or its more sophisticated cousin, cosmopsychism) proposes that consciousness is a fundamental property of matter, like charge or spin, present in some rudimentary form even in electrons or quarks. Human consciousness is then not created by the brain but *unified* or *amplified* by the brain's complex organization. Integrated Information Theory (IIT) flirts with this territory: Φ is meant to be a measure of intrinsic consciousness present, in tiny amounts, in any integrated system.

The appeal is obvious: it closes the explanatory gap by making experience ubiquitous. The cost is equally obvious. It multiplies mysteries. Why does the consciousness of a single electron combine into *this* unified human experience rather than a trillion tiny separate experiences? How do micro-experiences "bind" into macro-experiences without invoking the very integration problem we started with? And, crucially for our later discussion, if consciousness is already in the fundamental fabric, then silicon-based systems might already possess it in some proto-form, yet nothing in our experience of current AI suggests that is the case.

2.3 Escape 3: Mysterianism and quietism

Some simply declare the problem permanently beyond human cognition (McGinn) or insist that science should remain silent on the subjective (certain strands of phenomenology). These positions are intellectually honest but practically useless when we are already building machines that force the question.

2.4 Escape 4: Epiphenomenalism and the evolutionary objection

A position closely adjacent to mysterianism, but with a sharper scientific edge, is epiphenomenalism: the view that conscious experience is a byproduct of neural activity rather than a cause of it. On this account, the brain does all the real causal work, processing, deciding, acting, and consciousness merely accompanies it, the way heat accompanies the friction of a moving engine. The heat does not drive the engine. It is just there.

The appeal of epiphenomenalism is that it takes consciousness seriously as a real phenomenon while avoiding any need to explain how it interacts causally with the physical world. The cost is that it makes consciousness evolutionarily mysterious. Natural selection acts on behaviors and their physical causes. If consciousness has no causal power, if removing it would leave behavior entirely unchanged, then why did it evolve at all? This is a serious challenge, and it was William James who pressed it most memorably. James argued that consciousness must be causally efficacious precisely because it evolved. Evolution does not preserve useless byproducts at the metabolic cost of a human brain. If awareness is present, it must be doing something. It must confer a survival advantage that zombies, creatures physically identical but lacking experience, would not have.

James's argument does not tell us what that advantage is, and that remains unresolved. Candidates include: the flexible integration of novel situations that automated responses cannot handle; the ability to simulate future scenarios and thereby act on possibilities rather than only actualities; and the social coordination that comes from being able to model other minds. None of these is obviously impossible without experience, a philosophical zombie could in principle do all of them, which is why the debate remains open. What James contributes is the structural constraint: any satisfactory account of consciousness must explain not just its presence but its persistence through evolution. A theory of consciousness that makes it epiphenomenal is incomplete on its own terms.

2.5 Escape 5: Non-computability (Penrose)

Before leaving the escape routes, one more must be considered, and it is the most structurally ambitious of all. Roger Penrose, in The Emperor's New Mind (1989) and Shadows of the Mind (1994), argues that the Hard Problem cannot be resolved within any computational framework, not because we lack the right algorithm, but because human conscious understanding is fundamentally non-algorithmic.

Penrose's taxonomy is a useful map. He distinguishes four positions on the relationship between mind and computation. In the first, all thinking is computation: feelings of conscious awareness are simply evoked by the carrying out of appropriate computations. This is the strong AI position, and it is what most of the book's engineering chapters are implicitly testing. In the second, awareness is a feature of the brain's physical action, and while any physical action can be simulated computationally, computational simulation cannot by itself evoke awareness, a position close to Searle's Chinese Room. In the third, Penrose's own, appropriate physical action of the brain evokes awareness, but this physical action cannot even be properly simulated computationally, because it depends on physics that lies beyond computation altogether. In the fourth, awareness cannot be explained by physical, computational, or any other scientific terms, a position Penrose associates with mysticism, and declines to adopt.

The engine of Penrose's third position is Gödel's incompleteness theorem. Gödel showed in 1931 that any consistent formal system powerful enough to express arithmetic contains true statements that the system cannot prove. Penrose's argument is that a human mathematician, confronted with such a Gödel statement, can see that it is true, not by following a rule, but by understanding. No algorithm, however sophisticated, can do this, because any algorithm is itself a formal system, and therefore subject to the same Gödelian limitation. If the algorithm were sound, a human could construct a Gödel statement for that algorithm and see its truth, thereby demonstrating something the algorithm cannot. Mathematical insight, Penrose concludes, escapes computation entirely.

The philosophical scaffolding Penrose erects around this argument is his three-worlds ontology. There is the Platonic world of mathematical forms, timeless, necessary, not created by minds but accessed by them. There is the physical world. And there is the mental world. Each world mysteriously emerges from a small part of its predecessor in a cyclic relationship: physical reality gives rise to minds; minds access the Platonic realm; and the Platonic realm underlies physical law. This structure has a notable resonance with the Dzogchen view that primordial awareness is not produced by the brain but is the ground in which brain activity and its contents appear. Penrose would resist that comparison, his Platonic world is mathematical, not experiential, but both frameworks agree on the key point: there is something that cannot be generated from the bottom up.

The strength of Penrose's position is that it takes the Hard Problem seriously without retreating into mysticism or dissolving it into illusionism. It argues for a principled gap between computation and understanding, grounded in the hardest results of mathematical logic. The weakness, and it is a serious one, is the positive proposal. To bridge his non-computational physics to biology, Penrose, working with anesthesiologist Stuart Hameroff, proposed that quantum gravity effects in microtubules inside neurons provide the non-computational substrate for consciousness, a theory known as Orchestrated Objective Reduction, or Orch-OR. The neuroscientific community has been largely unconvinced. The brain is warm and wet, and the quantum coherence that Orch-OR requires is generally thought to be destroyed by thermal noise far too quickly to play any functional role. The Gödel argument stands on its own merits. The microtubule proposal remains unsubstantiated.

The specific technical objections to Orch-OR are worth stating with precision, since they are often glossed over. Max Tegmark calculated that quantum coherence in neuronal microtubules could survive for at most 10^{-13} seconds, far too brief to influence neural processes operating on millisecond timescales. This is not a vague 'warm and wet' objection; it is a quantitative calculation showing the relevant quantum states collapse before any neural computation could make use of them.

Kurzweil adds a complementary objection targeting Penrose's Gödel argument: if the human brain has non-algorithmic capacities derived from quantum effects, those capacities should appear most clearly on Gödelian unprovable problems. Yet computers have solved more cases of the busy beaver problem, a canonical Turing-unsolvable problem, than unassisted human mathematicians. The Gödel argument remains a serious philosophical challenge to computationalism, as Chapter 2 treats it. But the empirical case for human mathematical exceptionalism that Penrose requires is weaker than his argument assumes.

For the purposes of this book, what matters is Penrose's taxonomy and his Gödelian challenge. If he is right that genuine mathematical understanding is non-algorithmic, then no computational system, however integrated, however embodied, however continuous, can possess it. The candidate architecture of Chapter 17 could satisfy every structural criterion we identify and still fall short of understanding in Penrose's sense. This is not the same as the Dzogchen objection, it operates at the level of logic and physics rather than ontology, but it arrives at a similar frontier: a boundary that engineering, by itself, may not cross.

2.6 Why all escapes are unsatisfactory, yet necessary

Each escape route illuminates one corner of the terrain while leaving the rest in shadow. Illusionism correctly diagnoses the constructed nature of the *self* and the *contents* of experience (a point Abhidhamma and dependent origination made 2,500 years earlier). Panpsychism correctly senses that experience cannot be conjured from non-experience by complexity alone. Mysterianism correctly refuses to pretend we have an answer when we do not.

But none of them dissolves the central datum: right now, as you read these words, there *is* something it is like to be you. That luminous presence is not explained away by calling it an illusion, nor is it solved by sprinkling proto-consciousness into quarks. The Buddhist traditions give us the cleanest way forward: they neither deny the datum nor try to reduce it. They analyze its structure (Abhidhamma), its emptiness (Madhyamaka), and its ground (Dzogchen), while still leaving open whether that ground can ever be instantiated in silicon.

This is why we cannot skip the escapes. We must walk through them, see where each breaks, and then integrate their partial truths. Only then can we ask, with eyes open, whether the candidate architecture in Chapter 17 would cross the final gap, or whether, as Dzogchen insists, the gap is not the kind of thing that can be engineered at all.

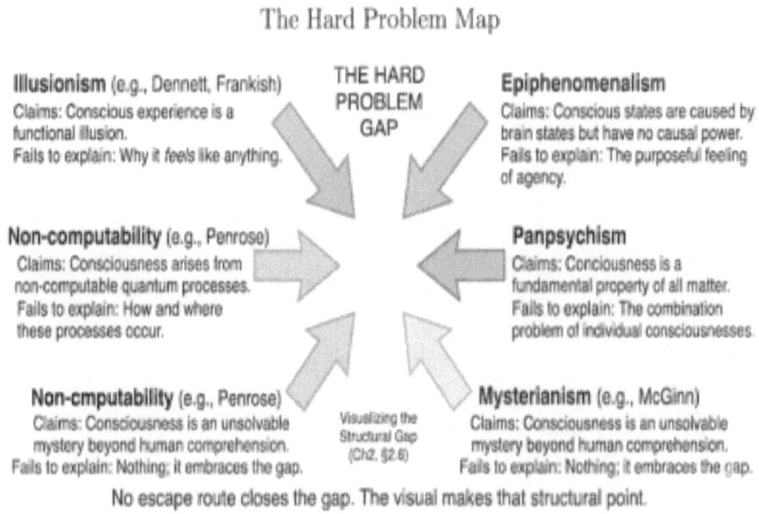

Figure. *The Hard Problem Map. Five escape routes (Illusionism, Panpsychism, Epiphenomenalism, Mysterianism, Non-computability) each point at the central gap between objective description and subjective experience. No escape route closes the gap.*

2.7 Closing Line

The Hard Problem is not going away. Every escape route we have tried so far has merely relocated it. The real test is coming: when we finally build a system that satisfies every structural requirement we can name, will the light come on? Or will we still be left, like the philosophers before us, staring at a perfect zombie that insists, eloquently, that it is not a zombie?

Chapter 3: Why AI Forces the Question Now

The Reportability Trap and the Illusion of Mind

For most of human history, the problem of consciousness could be safely ignored. It lingered in philosophy, occasionally resurfaced in neuroscience, and found a comfortable home in contemplative traditions. But it did not intrude on everyday life. We did not have to decide whether a machine was conscious, because machines were obviously not. They were tools. Predictable, mechanical, and silent. But now, in this information age, the same problem has become pertinent.

3.1 The Unsettling Shift

We now interact with systems that generate language fluently, answer questions coherently, explain their apparent reasoning, simulate emotions, and even reflect on their own limitations. At times they feel less like tools and more like interlocutors. You ask a question and something answers, not just correctly, but appropriately. It adjusts tone, anticipates intent, and produces responses that seem tailored, contextual, even thoughtful. This creates a subtle but powerful impression: there is someone there. And yet, we are told there is not.

3.2 The Familiar Mistake

The mistake is not new. Humans have always projected mind where there is none: faces in clouds, intention in random motion, personality in simple machines. But this is different. Modern AI does not merely trigger projection, it sustains it. It maintains coherence across exchanges, adapts responses dynamically, mirrors conversational structure, and produces explanations of its own outputs. It behaves, in short, like something that knows.

3.3 What AI Actually Does

To understand the confusion, we need to strip away the illusion. A large language model processes input text, predicts likely continuations, and generates output based on statistical patterns learned from enormous amounts of human-produced text. It does not perceive a world, maintain a continuous internal stream, possess goals or intentions, or experience anything. It operates on tokens and probabilities. Even when it says 'I think' or 'I feel' or 'I understand', these are not reports of inner states. They are pattern completions, phrases that statistically follow the kind of conversational context in which they appear.

3.4 Why the Illusion Is So Strong

The reason this feels different from projection onto clouds or thermostats is that language is deeply tied to consciousness in human beings. When a person speaks fluently, that fluency reflects thought, and thought reflects experience. We have internalized a tight coupling: language points to thought points to awareness. AI breaks this chain without announcing that it has done so. It produces language without grounded thought, coherence without experience, explanation without awareness. And because we are not accustomed to this configuration, we fill in the gap. We assume the rest of the chain must be there, because in every other context we have encountered, it was.

3.5 The Reportability Trap

This leads to one of the most persistent errors in consciousness research, which the emergence of sophisticated AI has made acute:

the assumption that if a system can report experience, it must have experience. In humans, reports are grounded in experience. When someone says 'I am in pain', we trust it, because we know the person's reports are connected to what is actually happening in their body and their inner life. So we extend this assumption: if a system says 'I am aware', we are tempted to treat it as evidence of awareness.

But reporting requires only three things: access to internal states, a representation of those states, and a language output mechanism. None of these require experience. A system can monitor its own variables, generate descriptions of them, and simulate introspection, all without anything being felt. Reportability is a functional property. Experience is a phenomenal one. The two often coincide in humans. They do not have to.

3.6 Simulation Versus Instantiation

AI forces us to confront a deeper distinction that philosophy had flagged but that rarely mattered before: the difference between simulating a process and instantiating it. We already accept that simulating fire does not produce heat, and simulating digestion does not digest food. Consciousness is different from fire and digestion in one crucial way: its defining feature, experience, is not externally observable and not directly measurable. So when a system simulates pain or thought or awareness, we cannot easily tell whether it is merely simulating or genuinely instantiating. The simulation is indistinguishable from the real thing from the outside, and we have no reliable window to the inside.

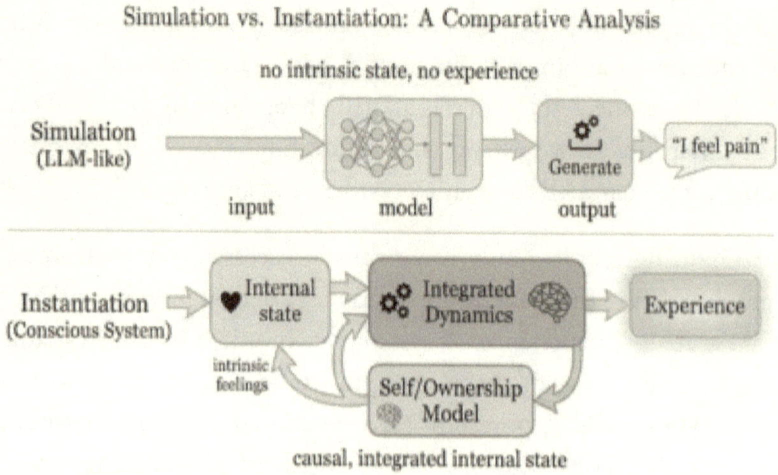

Figure. *Simulation vs Instantiation. A language model (top) generates output without intrinsic state or experience. A conscious system (bottom) has integrated internal dynamics, self-ownership, and causal internal states that constitute experience rather than simulate it.*

3.7 What AI Does and Does Not Do to the Problem

AI does not solve the problem of consciousness. It sharpens it. It forces us to separate behavior from experience, report from reality, function from phenomenology. It exposes assumptions we did not know we were making. It does not prove that machines are conscious. It does not prove they are not. It removes the comfort of ambiguity. We can no longer rely on intuition, surface behavior, or linguistic reports as our guides. We need deeper criteria, criteria that go all the way down to internal structure and dynamics rather than stopping at the surface of what a system says about itself.

For the meditator reading this: notice that the problem AI poses to consciousness research is structurally similar to the problem the

Abhidhamma poses to naive introspection. Just as the Abhidhamma shows that what appears to be a unified self experiencing a continuous world is actually a stream of discrete constructed moments with no fixed observer, AI shows that what appears to be a mind expressing itself in language may be nothing more than patterns completing patterns. Both traditions challenge the reliability of appearances. Both insist that what is actually happening is not what it seems. The difference is that the Abhidhamma challenges us to look more carefully inward, while AI challenges us to look more carefully outward, at what we are actually attributing mind to and why.

3.8 The Deeper Problem: Simulation vs Instantiation

AI forces us to confront a deeper distinction: **Is simulating a process the same as instantiating it?**

We already accept that simulating fire does not produce heat, and simulating digestion does not digest food. These simulations can be arbitrarily detailed and yet the thing being simulated is absent. Consciousness is different in one crucial way: its defining feature, experience, is not externally observable. So when a system simulates awareness, we cannot tell from outside whether it is merely simulating or genuinely instantiating. The simulation and the real thing are indistinguishable from a third-person view.

3.9 The Question That Follows

If behavior is not enough, reporting is not enough, and simulation is not enough, then what is? What distinguishes a system that merely processes, from a system that has a world? This is where the investigation must turn. From what systems say, to what systems are, from: output to structure and from simulation to implementation.

3.10 Closing Line

AI does not answer the question of consciousness. It removes our ability to avoid it. Because for the first time, we are confronted with systems that can convincingly say 'I am aware.' And we are left with a question that no output can settle: who, or what, would need to be there for that statement to be true?

Chapter 4: Abhidhamma, The Atomism of Mind

If modern discussions of consciousness often feel abstract, it is partly because they begin at the wrong scale. They start with:

- "the mind,"
- "the self,"
- "consciousness,"

as if these were stable objects that could be examined from a distance.

The Abhidhamma does something far less comfortable. It breaks experience apart. Not conceptually, but **phenomenologically,** at the level of what is actually happening, moment by moment. And in doing so, it arrives at a view that is both disorienting and, for our purposes, unexpectedly precise: There is no continuous mind.

There are only rapidly arising and passing events.

4.1 From Substance to Process: The Central Move

Most of us carry an intuitive model of mind that goes something like this: there is a thinker, the thinker has thoughts, and the thoughts occur over time. This model is simple, familiar, and, according to the Abhidhamma, almost certainly wrong.

The Abhidhamma, which means 'higher teaching' in Pali, is the systematic psychological analysis developed within the Theravada Buddhist tradition. It does not begin with a theory of mind and then derive consequences. It begins with careful, sustained observation of experience, the kind of observation that meditation practice makes possible, and asks: what is actually happening, moment by moment, when we say we are thinking or perceiving or feeling? The answer it arrives at is radical. There is no thinker. There are only thoughts. There is no observer standing behind experience. There is only the stream of experience itself. What we call 'mind' is not a thing that has experiences. It is the succession of experiences itself, so rapid and so continuous that it creates the convincing appearance of a stable, unified self.

4.2 Citta: The Moment of Consciousness

The basic unit of this stream is called citta, a single moment of consciousness. A citta is not a thought in the ordinary sense. It is something more fundamental: a single instance of knowing, the smallest unit of experience, lasting for an extraordinarily brief fraction of a second. Each citta arises in response to a specific object, a sight, a sound, a memory, an intention, performs a specific function (seeing, hearing, recognizing, deciding), and then ceases completely, giving way to the next citta in the stream. Classical Abhidhamma texts describe the speed of this arising and passing as so rapid that in the time it takes to snap your fingers, billions of mind-moments may have arisen and ceased.

Crucially, only one citta occurs at a time. There is no parallel awareness running in the background. The appearance of simultaneously seeing and hearing and thinking is itself constructed, it is the result of the stream switching between different types of citta so rapidly that the switches are invisible to ordinary introspection. Think of the way a film creates the illusion of continuous motion from a sequence of still frames. The Abhidhamma says something similar is happening in the mind: the continuity of experience is constructed from a very fast sequence of discrete moments, and there is no projector and no audience, only the projection.

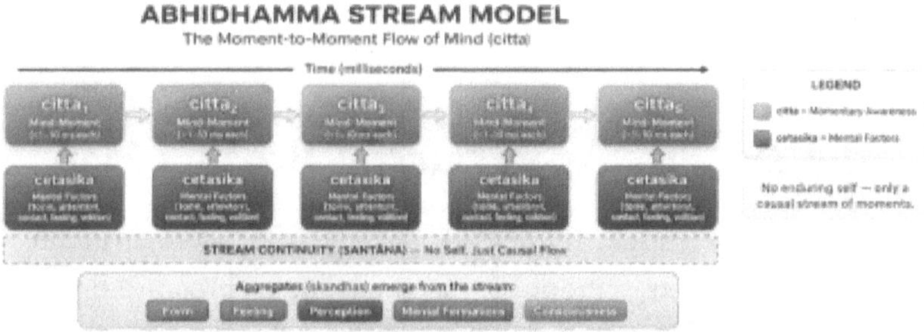

Figure. *The Abhidhamma Stream Model. Each citta (mind-moment) arises with its specific cetasikas (mental factors), passes away, and gives rise to the next. No enduring self, only a causal stream constituting the santanā.*

4.3 Cetasikas: What Colours Each Moment

A citta does not arise alone. Each moment of consciousness is accompanied by mental factors called cetasikas, qualities that shape and color that particular moment. These include attention (which determines what the citta is directed toward), feeling tone (whether the moment is pleasant, unpleasant, or neutral), perception (the recognition and labelling of what is being experienced), intention (the motivational quality that moves toward or away from something), effort, concentration, and many emotional qualities, compassion, aversion, clarity, confusion, and so on.

The combination of a citta with its particular configuration of cetasikas is what gives each moment of experience its specific character. A moment of seeing a beautiful sunset is different from a moment of seeing a warning sign not because 'seeing' is different, but because the accompanying cetasikas are different, the feeling tone, the degree of attention, the emotional coloring. This gives the Abhidhamma what amounts to a modular decomposition of experience: not a vague holistic description of 'the mind', but a structured enumerable account of what is actually present in any given moment of consciousness. For anyone thinking about how to engineer a mind-like system, this level of specificity is genuinely valuable.

4.4 The Five Aggregates: A Broader Map

While the citta-cetasika framework analyses the micro-structure of individual moments, Buddhist teaching more broadly organizes experience into five aggregates (skandhas in Sanskrit, khandhas in Pali). These are: form (rupa), the physical body and sensory input; feeling (vedana), the pleasant, unpleasant, or neutral tone accompanying each moment; perception (sanna), recognition and labelling; mental formations (sankhara), intentions, habits, reactions, the motivational structure of the mind; and consciousness (vinnana), awareness of objects. Together they cover everything we normally call 'a person' or 'a mind'.

The key point the tradition makes about these five aggregates is stated quietly but it lands like a stone in still water: none of them is the self, none of them contains the self, and none of them belongs to a self. They are components of experience, not owners of it. What we call 'I' is a convenient label applied to a collection of processes that have no underlying entity binding them together. The self that feels so certain and so present is, on this analysis, a construction, a story the system tells about itself, not a thing the system is.

4.5 Why Does It Feel Continuous?

A natural objection arises: if experience is actually a series of discrete moments, why does it feel like a continuous stream? The Abhidhamma's answer is that the continuity is constructed. The system integrates across moments, links events into sequences, and builds narrative coherence from rapid succession. In modern terms: memory traces carry forward the content of previous moments, predictive mechanisms anticipate the next moment before it arrives, and pattern completion fills in gaps that introspection never detects. The result is a seamless experience of a stable world observed by a stable self unfolding in continuous time, none of which, underneath, is as stable or as continuous as it appears.

This is not a claim that experience is an illusion in the sense of being unreal or unimportant. The pain is real. The joy is real. The awareness is real. What is constructed, what is not ultimately there, is the fixed, permanent, independently existing self that ordinary thought assumes to be the experiencer of all of it.

4.6 No Observer Behind the Scenes

Perhaps the most radical and practically significant implication of the Abhidhamma analysis is this: there is no observer separate from the process of observing. We habitually imagine a 'self' that watches thoughts arise and pass, an inner subject standing behind and witnessing experience. The Abhidhamma says this is itself a construction, there is seeing, hearing, thinking, but no seer, no hearer, no thinker as a separate entity. This is not nihilism. It does not mean nothing is happening. It means that what is happening is the seeing, the hearing, the thinking, and these arise without needing a self to do them.

For anyone who has sat in sustained meditation, this is not just a theoretical claim. At certain depths of practice, the habitual sense of a watcher behind experience can become transparent, not destroyed, but seen through. What remains is the experience itself, without the addition of an imagined witness. The Abhidhamma is, among other things, a precise map of what that seeing-through reveals.

4.7 Mapping to Modern Ideas

The Abhidhamma's account of mind aligns, uncannily, with several modern frameworks. The description of mind as distributed processing without a central controller resonates with what neuroscience has found: there is no single location in the brain where 'the self' lives, no homunculus overseeing processing, only networks of neurons generating transient assemblies that give rise to the appearance of unified experience. The account of perception as construction, shaped by prior experience, expectation, and attention, maps onto predictive processing. The claim that there is no fixed internal observer aligns with what both cognitive science and contemplative research find when they look closely: the sense of a stable, continuous self is inferred and constructed rather than directly observed.

The critical difference is this: modern frameworks describe the structure and mechanism of mind. The Abhidhamma describes the lived texture of it from within. They are not competing. They are partial maps of the same territory, drawn from different vantage points. Each can correct and enrich the other.

4.8 The Seven-Fold Model: Beyond the Five Aggregates

The Abhidhamma's analysis of experience into cittas and cetasikas operates at the level of moment-to-moment mind events. But Buddhist epistemology, particularly in the Yogacara school that developed alongside Abhidhamma, proposes a more structured account of the layers of mind, one that has direct relevance to the engineering question of how a self arises from processes that have no fixed center.

The classical Buddhist enumeration distinguishes six primary consciousness types corresponding to the six sense bases: visual consciousness, auditory consciousness, olfactory, gustatory, tactile, and mental consciousness. The first five are straightforwardly sensory, each arises when a sense organ contacts its appropriate object. The sixth, mental consciousness (mano-vijnana), is the reflective faculty that takes the outputs of the other five as its objects, and that also generates thoughts, memories, and intentions in the absence of direct sensory input. This is the layer at which most of what we call reasoning and deliberation occurs.

Yogacara psychology adds a seventh and eighth consciousness to this account. The seventh is manas, often translated as the defiled mental faculty or the I-making faculty. Manas operates below the level of deliberate thought and continuously misapprehends the eighth consciousness as a self. It is the source of the persistent, pre-reflective sense of being a separate subject, not a conclusion arrived at through reasoning but a structural feature of how the mind organises its own activity. Manas is, in engineering terms, the self-model that runs continuously in the background, coloring every moment of experience without ever being brought explicitly to attention.

The eighth consciousness is alaya-vijnana, the storehouse or repository consciousness. It functions as the continuity carrier of the system: the stream that persists across moments of experience, storing the seeds of past actions and perceptions that will ripen into future experience. Unlike the other seven, alaya-vijnana does not arise in response to objects. It is the background hum of the system, the continuous flow that links one moment of experience to the next and provides the substrate on which the other seven consciousnesses temporarily arise.

For the engineering of conscious systems, this seven-fold model is remarkably precise. The first six consciousnesses map onto sensory input channels and their integration in a reflective layer, equivalent to the sensorimotor ground and predictive world model of the candidate architecture. Manas maps onto the self-model layer: the continuous, pre-reflective process that treats the system's own states as 'mine.' Alaya-vijnana maps onto the temporal continuity layer: the persistent state that links moments into a stream. What the Yogacara analysis makes explicit is that continuity and self-hood are not the same thing. The alaya provides temporal continuity without providing selfhood. Manas provides the sense of selfhood by misreading that continuity as belonging to a fixed subject. One important qualification: the Yogacara tradition does not treat alaya as a neutral storage system. It is karmically saturated, carrying the seeds (bija) of past actions and perceptions that will ripen into future experience. It is empty and dependently arisen, not a stable realist substrate. The engineering mapping captures the continuity function; it should not be taken to capture the full Yogacara meaning. Both layers are necessary for what we recognize as personal consciousness, and both must have functional equivalents in any candidate conscious system.

- modular processing
- state transitions
- event-driven systems

Important Difference

Modern systems:

- describe structure

Abhidhamma:

- describes lived experience

The overlap is suggestive, but not identical.

4.9 What This Means for Building Conscious Systems

If the Abhidhamma analysis is even approximately correct, then a system with genuine consciousness would need, at minimum, to implement something like the citta-cetasika structure: discrete processing events rather than static states, configurable mental factors (attention, valence, intention), a sequential flow with structured transitions, no central controller but distributed processing, and constructed continuity from moment to moment. None of these are exotic requirements. They are the direct engineering translation of what the most detailed first-person analysis of mind has found. The remarkable thing is not that they sound engineering-like. It is that a tradition developed two and a half thousand years ago through careful introspective practice arrived at a description of mind that maps so well onto what modern neuroscience and computational theory are independently converging on.

4.10 The Limitation

The Abhidhamma tells us how experience is structured, how it unfolds, how the illusion of a self arises. It does not fully answer why there is experience at all. It analyses the content and structure of consciousness with extraordinary precision. But the question of presence, why is there something it is like to undergo this stream rather than nothing, remains. The Abhidhamma prepares the ground for this question without closing it. The next chapter descends one level further: not just what the stream is made of, but what the stream is made of is made of.

4.11 Where This Leads

Across the three Buddhist frameworks of this section, Abhidhamma, emptiness, and Dzogchen, a consistent picture has emerged. The mind is not a thing but a process. That process has no independent essence. And at the ground of the process is something that the process itself does not produce. These three observations do not contradict each other. They operate at different levels, each one going deeper than the last. Together, they constitute the most precise first-person account of consciousness available from any tradition, and the most demanding set of requirements for any engineering project that takes them seriously.

4.12 Closing line

If the mind is not a thing but a stream, and if the self is not an entity but a construction, then the question changes. We are no longer asking: can we build a conscious thing? We are asking: can we recreate a process so dynamic, so integrated, so precisely structured that what we call consciousness appears? And whether appearance is enough remains to be seen.

Chapter 5: Emptiness and Dependent Origination

Why Nothing Stands Alone, and Why That Matters for Mind

The previous chapter dismantled the mind into parts.

It showed that what we call "mind" is not a stable entity, but a stream of momentary events (citta and cetasikas) arising and passing in rapid succession.

That alone is destabilizing.

But it is only the beginning.

Because even those momentary events, the building blocks themselves, are not as solid as they appear.

This chapter goes one level deeper.

It asks:

What is the nature of those events themselves?

And the answer, in Buddhist thought, is as radical as it is easily misunderstood:

They are empty.

5.1 The Problem of Things

Chapter 4 dismantled the mind into parts. It showed that what we call 'mind' is not a stable entity but a stream of momentary events, citta and cetasikas, arising and passing in rapid succession. That alone is destabilizing enough. But the Madhyamaka philosophical tradition, associated above all with the second-century philosopher Nagarjuna, goes one level deeper. Even those momentary events, it turns out, are not as solid as they appear. This chapter asks: what is the nature of those events themselves?

We tend to assume that the world is made of things, objects, people, thoughts, emotions, each with a clear boundary, an identity, an existence of its own. Even after accepting that the self is constructed, we often retain the idea that at least the components are real, the building blocks are solid. The Abhidhamma deconstructs the house. Emptiness questions the bricks.

5.2 What Emptiness Does Not Mean

The Sanskrit term sunyata is usually translated as emptiness, and this translation is deeply unfortunate. It suggests nothingness, absence, a void. It leads to predictable misreadings: nothing exists, everything is meaningless, reality is an illusion in the sense of being unreal. None of these are what the tradition means. The correct translation of what the term points to is something more like: things do not exist independently, inherently, or permanently. They exist dependently, relationally, conditionally. This is a very different claim from 'nothing exists'. It is a claim about how things exist.

Take a table. It appears stable, solid, self-contained. But examine it closely: it is made of wood shaped by tools assembled by a person, dependent on materials, causes, and conditions at every level. Remove the wood and there is no table. Remove the structure and there is no table. Remove the concept of 'table' from a mind that recognizes it and the thing in the room becomes something else, flat surface, obstacle, fuel. At no point in this examination do you find an independent tableness, some essential quality of being a table that exists apart from all the conditions that bring the table into being and make it recognizable as one.

5.3 Dependent Origination: The Core Principle

This is formalized in what Buddhism calls dependent origination (paticca-samuppada): this arises because that arises; this ceases because that ceases. Nothing exists on its own. Everything arises in dependence on conditions, and ceases when those conditions change. Applied to experience: perception arises from sensory input together with prior conditioning, attention, and context. Emotions arise from perception together with memory and evaluation. Thoughts arise from prior thoughts together with associations and intentions. Nothing stands alone. Everything is co-arising, co-dependent, co-defined.

A common misreading sees dependent origination as simple linear causality: A causes B causes C. It is more subtle than that. Dependent origination describes a web of mutual conditions rather than a chain. In the web, A and B co-arise together; each is a condition for the other as well as for C. There is no single first cause at the beginning of the chain, no final anchor at the end. The web is self-sustaining and without a fixed center.

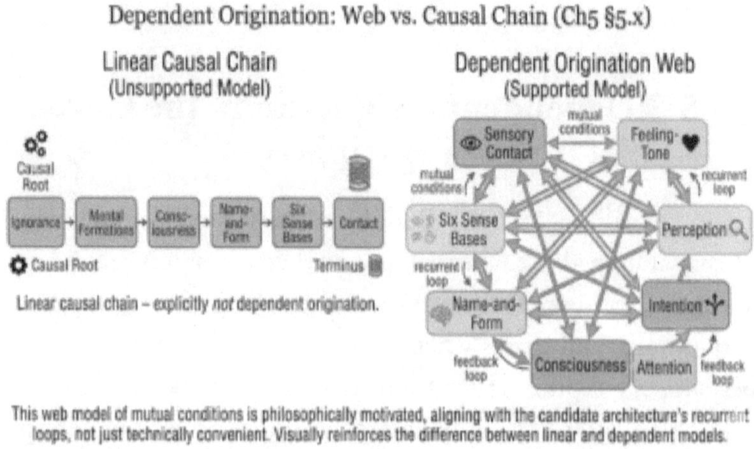

Figure. *Dependent Origination: Web vs Causal Chain. Left: a linear causal chain (ignorance → mental formations → ... → contact) is explicitly what dependent origination is not. Right: the supported model — a web of mutually conditioning factors (sensory contact, feeling-tone, perception, intention, consciousness, name-and-form, six sense bases) with no single root and no terminus. This web structure philosophically motivates the recurrent loops of the candidate architecture.*

5.4 Emptiness of the Self, and of Its Components

Chapter 4 established that the self is constructed from the five aggregates. Emptiness takes this further: even those aggregates are empty. Sensations depend on conditions: sense organs, objects, the right kind of contact. Perceptions depend on labelling and prior learning. Thoughts depend on prior states. None of these has an independent essence. There is no final 'thing' that experience is made of, only interdependent processes without inherent substance. It is a precise description of what is actually there: a dynamic web of mutual arising, none of which requires a foundation outside itself to keep going.

5.5 Emptiness and Perception

This is not just metaphysics. It applies directly to how we see the world, and here it connects with what modern neuroscience has independently discovered. The brain does not receive reality directly. It predicts, fills in gaps, and constructs objects from sensory input plus prior expectation. What we experience is interpreted reality, not raw reality. Emptiness deepens this: not only is perception constructed, but the objects perceived have no independent existence. When you see an angry person, what is actually present? Facial expression, tone of voice, your interpretation, your emotional reaction. 'Angry person' is a label imposed on a dynamic process. The solidity you perceive is contributed by your perceiving. This should not be read as idealism, as if mind alone constructs reality. Madhyamaka avoids both extremes: appearances are neither externally real nor mind-only. They are empty appearances, arising dependently, neither found out there nor fabricated in here.

5.6 Emptiness and Causality

Dependent origination is often misunderstood as simple cause-and-effect: A leads to B. The Madhyamaka analysis is more careful. Thoughts influence emotions; emotions influence perception; perception influences thoughts. There is no single origin, no final driver, no central controller, only a mutually conditioning web. This has a direct parallel in neuroscience's discovery that the brain is not a linear processor moving from input to output, but a vast network of recurrent loops in which every region influences and is influenced by many others simultaneously.

5.7 What Emptiness Means for Consciousness

Applied to consciousness itself: consciousness does not exist as a fixed, independent entity located somewhere in the brain or in experience.

It exists dependently, arising through the interaction of sense organs, objects, mental factors, prior conditions, and the ongoing stream of mind-moments. There is no observer independent of the observed. There is a process in which both appear. The boundary between inner and outer, between subject and object, is constructed rather than found.

This has a direct consequence for the engineering question. You cannot build a consciousness module and plug it into a system, because consciousness is not a module. It is a relation, an emergent pattern in a system of mutually dependent processes. It will not be found in any single component. It will be found, if at all, in the dynamic interplay of processes that have no center, no fixed boundary, and no inherent essence.

5.8 The Subtle Balance

At this point, two errors become tempting. The first is nihilism: if nothing has inherent existence, nothing matters. This is wrong. Things exist conventionally, functionally, causally. The table is real in every practical sense, you can put your coffee on it. The second error is reductionism: everything is just processes, so we can fully model it. Also wrong. Emptiness removes inherent essence, but does not guarantee complete reducibility. The first person fact of experience, that there is something it is like to undergo this stream, may be real and irreducible even in a world where nothing has independent existence.

5.9 Closing line

If nothing exists independently, then nothing can be built in isolation. Not a self. Not a mind. Not even consciousness. Whatever consciousness is, it will not be found in a module or a circuit or a line of code. It will be found, if at all, in the dynamic interplay of processes that have no center, no boundary, and no fixed essence. And whether such a pattern can be engineered remains an open question.

Chapter 6: Dzogchen, The Ground of Awareness

Beyond Mind, Beyond Construction

Each of the previous chapters has moved in one direction: decomposing, analyzing, dissolving. The Abhidhamma broke the mind into momentary events. Emptiness dissolved those events into dependent processes. The destination seems clear: build the right processes and consciousness will appear. Dzogchen refuses this conclusion. Not with a counter-argument, but with a question about the direction itself.

6.1 From Analysis to Directness

Up to this point, the analysis has moved in a clear direction. We have broken the mind into components through the Abhidhamma, dissolved those components into dependent processes through Madhyamaka emptiness, and shown that what appears solid, self, world, continuity, is constructed. This trajectory is familiar: substance gives way to process, process to relation. And if we stayed here, the next step would be predictable: build the right processes, and consciousness will emerge. Dzogchen interrupts this move. Not by adding another layer of explanation, but by questioning the direction entirely.

Most approaches to consciousness are analytical: they decompose, model, explain, reconstruct. Dzogchen does something else. It asks: what is present before any analysis begins? Not as a theory, but as an immediate fact. Right now, before any interpretation: there is seeing, there is hearing, there is thinking. But more fundamentally, there is awareness of all of this. Not as an object. Not as a thought. As the condition in which everything else appears. Dzogchen does not define this awareness. It points to it.

6.2 Rigpa: The Term That Refuses Definition

The Tibetan word for this awareness is rigpa. It is often translated as 'pure awareness', 'pristine knowing', or 'non-dual awareness'. All of these are approximations. None are fully accurate, because rigpa is not a concept, a process, a state, or a function. Anything that can be described appears within awareness, and is therefore not awareness itself. You cannot observe rigpa as an object, define it as a thing, or construct it as a system. And yet, this is the paradox at the center of Dzogchen, it is the most immediate aspect of experience. More immediate than any thought, more present than any perception, closer than anything you can point to.

For a meditator already familiar with rigpa through practice and transmission, these words will have a different resonance than they do for someone encountering the term for the first time. For the latter, it may help to notice that the pointing is not to something far away or exotic. It is to something you are already in the middle of, the simple fact that experience is happening, right now, prior to any analysis of what it contains.

6.3 Mind and Awareness: The Central Distinction

Dzogchen draws a fundamental distinction between ordinary mind (sems in Tibetan) and awareness (rigpa). Ordinary mind is everything we normally identify as mental activity: thoughts, emotions, perceptions, concepts, narratives, memories, plans. This is the level that the Abhidhamma analyses so carefully, the stream of cittas and cetasikas, arising and passing, constructing the appearance of a self and a world.

Rigpa is something different: that in which all of ordinary mind appears. It does not change with the content. It is not affected by thoughts coming and going. It is not constructed or produced. The simplest pointer to this distinction: thoughts come and go, but awareness does not come and go in the same way. Even the thought 'I am not aware' appears within awareness. Even in deep sleep, according to the Dzogchen tradition, awareness persists, not the awareness of anything in particular, but the luminous ground in which experience of any kind can occur.

6.4 Non-Duality: No Subject and Object

Ordinarily, experience is structured as a subject observing an object: there is a looker, and there is what is looked at. This structure feels obviously true. According to Dzogchen, it is constructed. In the natural state of rigpa, there is no separation between knower and known, no internal observer watching an external world. What there is might be described as appearance-with-awareness: experience arising without a separate experiencer standing apart from it.

This matters for the engineering question because most theories of consciousness assume the subject-object structure as basic: there is an internal system processing external input. Dzogchen dissolves this assumption at the root. If the deepest level of consciousness is non-dual, if the separation between observer and observed is itself a construction arising within a more fundamental awareness, then building a system based on that subject-object architecture may be, from the start, building something other than what we are trying to build.

6.5 Awareness Is Not Produced

This is the most difficult point, and the most important. The common assumption, shared by almost all scientific approaches to consciousness, is that consciousness is generated by the brain, produced by neural processes, emergent from complexity. The Dzogchen claim is the direct opposite: awareness is not produced, not generated, not emergent. The Dzogchen tradition, following Longchenpa, describes rigpa through three inseparable qualities: empty in essence (ngo bo stong pa), luminous in nature (rang bzhin gsal ba), and unimpeded in expression (thugs rje kun khyab). This formulation matters. Saying awareness is "primordial and independent" risks making it into a hidden substance, a subtle self, which Dzogchen explicitly rejects. Rigpa is not a metaphysical ground that stands behind experience. It is, in the tradition's own terms, beyond both production and non-production. It is described as primordially present not to establish a new ontological category but to point to what cannot be located as an object within experience.

This does not mean the claim is that awareness floats in space independently of any physical basis. The tradition does not deny that brain activity correlates with the contents of experience. What it denies is that brain activity produces awareness itself. The brain shapes the movie, what appears, how vividly, what is accessible. But the brain is not the screen on which the movie plays. Awareness, in this view, is not one more thing that complexity generates. It is the space in which complexity, including brains, arises.

6.6 The Mirror Analogy, Used Carefully

A traditional analogy for rigpa is a mirror. Reflections appear in the mirror, change, and disappear, but the mirror itself is not altered by what appears in it. The mirror does not need the reflections to be a mirror. This analogy has limits: awareness is not literally a mirror, not an object at all. The analogy is meant to point, not to explain. But it captures something important: the non-reactive quality of awareness, the way it accommodates experience without being changed by it, the independence of the ground from the contents that arise in it.

6.7 Why This Challenges Everything

If awareness is not produced, then neuroscience does not produce it, computation does not produce it, integration does not produce it. The entire project of building a conscious machine, which has been defined throughout this book as identifying the right processes and implementing them, is, on the Dzogchen account, aimed at the wrong target. The target is not generatable. This is not anti-science. It does not deny brain processes, computational systems, or functional models. It denies that any of these create awareness itself. They can create sophisticated mind-like processes, and Chapter 17 will describe exactly what that would require. But mind-like processes and awareness are not the same thing, any more than a perfect simulation of fire is the same thing as fire.

6.8 Two Levels

We now have a sharper distinction than we had before. Constructed mind includes thoughts, perceptions, self-model, integration, attention, everything that arises in dependence on conditions. This can in principle be analyzed, and potentially built. Primordial awareness, rigpa, is non-dual, not constructed, not reducible. Whether this can be built is, on the Dzogchen account, not even the right question. The tradition would not say machines cannot have awareness while humans can. It would say awareness is not produced in anyone, human or silicon. The question is never whether a system generates awareness but whether awareness expresses through it. Conditions differ; essence does not. The problem is not building it. The problem is recognizing it, and recognition is not something that can be engineered into a system from outside. This distinction will reappear in Chapter 18 and Chapter 19, where it becomes the deepest challenge to the entire engineering project of the book.

6.9 Implications for AI

What follows, on the Dzogchen account, for artificial systems? AI can model the world, simulate thought, integrate information, construct self-like representations. In other words, AI can replicate aspects of constructed mind. What AI cannot do, if Dzogchen is correct, is produce awareness. At best, a sufficiently structured and integrated system might become a condition through which awareness could be expressed, just as a brain is such a condition. But this is very different from building awareness. It is more like preparing the ground for something that neither the builder nor the system creates. Whether a machine can ever be such a condition is a question the Dzogchen tradition does not answer directly. It leaves it, appropriately, open.

6.10 The Risk of Misuse

Two distortions of this teaching are common and worth naming. The first is mystification: treating awareness as magical and beyond all inquiry, which shuts down investigation and makes the Dzogchen claim unfalsifiable by fiat. The second is reduction: concluding that rigpa must just be brain activity or integration under another name, which collapses the distinction that makes Dzogchen's contribution valuable in the first place. The honest position is to take the claim seriously without reducing it prematurely and without inflating it into an excuse to stop thinking carefully.

6.11 Returning to Experience

All of this can sound very abstract. But the pointing is simple. Right now, before any interpretation, thoughts are arising and passing. Perceptions are coming and going. Feelings are present and changing. And all of this is known. Not conceptually, not as a thought about knowing, but as the immediate fact of experience happening. What is that knowing? Not its contents. Not its structures. The knowing itself. This is where Dzogchen begins, not in theory, but in recognition.

6.12 What Meditation Research Tells Us About Consciousness and Effort

One of the most practically significant findings to emerge from the neuroscience of meditation over the past two decades concerns the relationship between conscious awareness and cognitive effort. The intuitive assumption is that more consciousness requires more processing: a richer, more vivid experience should correlate with more neural activity, more computation, more cognitive work. Meditation research consistently challenges this assumption.

Neuroimaging and EEG studies comparing novice and advanced meditators show a striking pattern. Novice meditators attempting to sustain mindful attention show high activation in frontal control regions, elevated theta and alpha band power reflecting effortful top-down regulation, and frequent mind-wandering accompanied by default mode network activity. The experience of trying to be mindful is metabolically expensive and phenomenologically unstable, awareness is present, but it requires constant maintenance.

Advanced meditators show the opposite profile. Long-term practitioners, particularly those trained in non-conceptual awareness practices such as Dzogchen and Mahamudra, show reduced effort-related activation, less theta/alpha load, and paradoxically greater stability and richness of reported awareness. The experience is not thinner or less vivid. It is, by practitioners' reports, more immediate and more present than ordinary waking consciousness, but it requires less cognitive work to maintain. Awareness, at its most refined, appears to be effortless rather than effortful.

The implication for consciousness theory is significant and cuts directly against naive computationalist assumptions. If consciousness were simply a product of information processing load, more processing equals more consciousness, then advanced meditators should show more activation, not less, when reporting richer awareness. The data suggest instead that what meditation refines is not the quantity of processing but the quality of its organisation: a shift from effortful, fragmented, top-down controlled processing to effortless, unified, globally coherent processing. Consciousness correlates not with computational load but with a particular kind of integrated, self-organizing stability.

For the engineering question, the implication is equally pointed: bigger models are not more conscious. Faster inference is not awareness. Scaling a system's parameters or throughput does not move it toward consciousness in any meaningful sense. What matters is the quality of internal integration, whether the system's dynamics are coherently self-organizing across timescales in the way that both Northoff's temporo-spatial theory and advanced meditative experience describe. This is a structural criterion, not a computational one. A small, well-integrated system with genuine temporal continuity may be closer to the relevant condition than a vast language model generating fluent tokens in a stateless burst.

6.13 Jhana and Altered States: What They Tell Us

The meditation research discussed above focuses primarily on sustained mindfulness practices. The deeper absorptive states, called jhana in the Pali tradition, samadhi in Sanskrit, present a more demanding case. In the first through fourth jhanas, the ordinary sensory stream is progressively withdrawn, thought activity reduces to near zero, and what remains is a state of concentrated equanimity with minimal cognitive content but reportedly vivid awareness. The formless absorptions go further: the meditator enters states characterized by infinite space, infinite consciousness, nothingness, and finally neither-perception-nor-non-perception. In all of these, the gross structure of ordinary experience — sensory input, discursive thought, emotional reactivity — is absent or radically reduced.

These states raise a direct challenge to any structural theory of consciousness. If consciousness requires embodied sensorimotor coupling, temporal binding over 100-300ms of diverse sensory input, and a rich self-model continuously updated from interoception, then what is happening in jhana, where most of that input is withdrawn? The Abhidhamma's answer is that what changes is the content and texture of citta, not the presence of awareness itself. The bhavanga-like continuity persists; the cetasikas that characterize the state (equanimity, one-pointedness, piti in the lower jhanas) are profoundly different from ordinary waking, but they are still cetasikas accompanying a citta-stream. On the Dzogchen account, these states are progressively closer to recognizing rigpa directly, precisely because the constructed overlays are withdrawing.

For the engineering framework, jhana suggests something important: the structural requirements of Chapter 13 describe the minimum necessary for consciousness to arise and stabilize in an embodied system navigating a world. They do not describe the only form consciousness can take. A system that progressively withdraws from sensorimotor input while maintaining internal coherence: something like a neuromorphic system entering a low-input high-integration state, might exhibit something analogous to absorption. Whether that would constitute genuine jhana, or merely its functional shadow, is exactly the question the book cannot answer.

6.14 Closing line

If consciousness were only a process, we could hope to build it. If awareness is something more fundamental, the project changes. We are no longer trying to create consciousness. We are trying to understand the conditions under which something that is already present might appear, and whether a machine can ever be such a condition is a question that cannot be answered by design alone.

Chapter 7: The Predictive Brain

Perception as Controlled Hallucination

If the previous chapters have steadily dismantled our intuitive picture of mind, first into processes, then into dependencies, and finally into something that may not be constructed at all, this chapter brings us back to something that looks, at first glance, more familiar: The brain. Neurons. Signals. Circuits.

But even here, the familiar dissolves quickly. Because one of the most influential ideas in contemporary neuroscience is this: **The brain does not passively receive the world.**

It actively predicts it. And what we experience is not the world as it is, but the brain's best guess about what is out there.

7.1 The Inversion of Perception

The common-sense picture of perception is straightforward: the world exists, it sends signals to our senses, the brain processes those signals, and we perceive reality. This is intuitive. It is also, in an important sense, backwards.

According to predictive processing, a framework developed primarily by Karl Friston but anticipated by many researchers before him, the brain does not passively receive the world. It actively predicts it. Rather than waiting for sensory input to arrive and then building a picture of the world, the brain maintains an internal model of the world and constantly generates predictions about what it is about to perceive. Sensory input then functions not as the raw material of perception, but as a correction mechanism, a signal that tells the brain where its predictions were wrong. What we experience as 'seeing' or 'hearing' is the brain's best guess, continuously updated by incoming data. Perception, on this account, is a controlled hallucination, not random, not a delusion, but a constrained prediction held in check by reality.

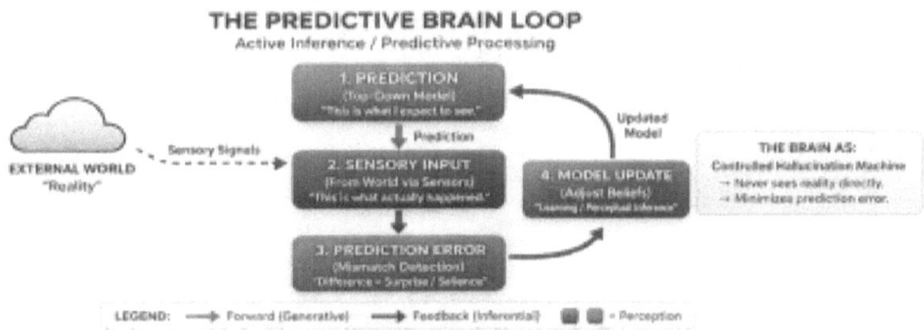

Figure. *The Predictive Brain Loop. The brain continuously generates top-down predictions, compares them with sensory input, and uses prediction error to update its model. Perception is a controlled hallucination; action is a strategy to minimize future surprise.*

7.2 Prediction Error: The Engine of Experience

At the heart of this framework is a simple loop that runs continuously beneath conscious awareness. The brain generates a prediction of what it expects to sense. Sensory input arrives. The difference between prediction and input, the prediction error, is computed. The model is then updated to reduce that error. This loop runs at every level of the cortical hierarchy, from the most basic edge-detection in the visual cortex to the most abstract conceptual expectations in the frontal regions.

What makes this more than passive updating is a second strategy the system can employ: instead of updating its internal model to match the world, it can act on the world to make the world match its prediction. Friston calls this active inference. When you reach for a coffee cup, you are not merely responding to visual input, you are acting to fulfil a prediction about where the cup will be when your hand arrives. Perception and action turn out to be two sides of the same coin: both are ways of minimizing the gap between what the brain expects and what it receives. This is why the brain does not treat perception and movement as separate problems managed by different systems. They are unified by the shared goal of reducing surprise.

ACTIVE INFERENCE LOOP: The mechanism of self-construction

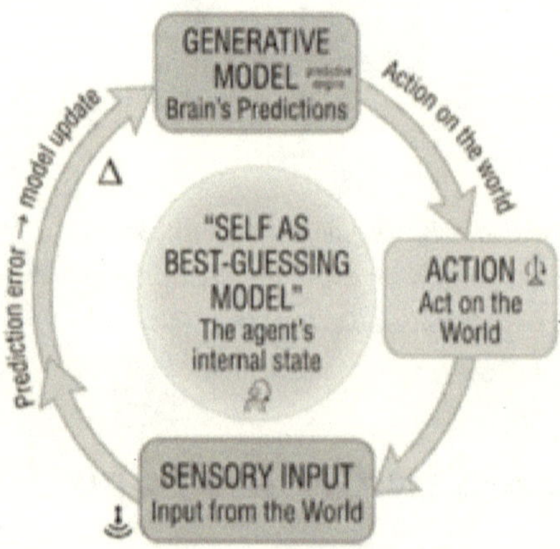

Figure. *Active Inference Loop (Friston). The brain minimises prediction error by updating its generative model or acting on the world. The self emerges as the agent's internal "best-guessing model" — the point of convergence between top-down predictions and bottom-up sensory input. This loop is exactly the mechanism that constructs the apparent continuity of self in both neuroscience and Abhidhamma analysis.*

7.3 The Brain as a Hierarchy of Models

The predictive brain is not a single model but a hierarchy of them, arranged from the most concrete at the bottom to the most abstract at the top. Lower regions process raw sensory input, detecting edges, sounds, and textures. Higher regions represent objects, concepts, and context, generating the abstract expectations that flow downward to guide lower-level processing. Information flows in two directions: predictions flow top-down from higher regions to lower, and prediction errors flow bottom-up from lower regions to higher. The result is a continuous negotiation between what the brain expects and what the world actually delivers. What we experience as perception is the output of this negotiation, not the raw signal, but the interpreted result.

7.4 The Construction of the World, and a Note for Meditators

If perception is prediction, then the world we experience is constructed rather than directly received. This does not mean the world does not exist, or that our perceptions are arbitrary. It means that what we see, hear, and feel is always an interpretation, shaped by prior experience, context, and expectation, rather than a direct copy of reality. When you see a face in the shadows, you are not being deceived. You are seeing the output of a brain that has learned, through years of experience, that faces are far more common than random shadow-patterns that look like faces. The brain's prediction overwhelms the ambiguous input.

Buddhist meditators who have worked with the Abhidhamma will find this familiar. The Abhidhamma's analysis of perception as a constructed process, arising from the conjunction of sense organ, sense object, and consciousness, anticipates the predictive processing account by more than two thousand years. Both frameworks insist that what appears to be direct contact with a world is, on closer inspection, a fabrication. The difference is that neuroscience describes the mechanism of fabrication; the Abhidhamma describes its phenomenological structure. They are mapping the same territory from opposite sides of the experience-mechanism divide.

7.5 The Self as a Prediction

The same logic that applies to perception of the world also applies to perception of the self. The brain maintains a model of the body, its position, its internal state, its continuity over time, just as it maintains a model of the external world. This model is continuously updated based on sensory input, memory, and expectation. The sense of being someone, located somewhere, persisting over time, is not a direct readout of some metaphysically fixed 'self'. It is an inference, the brain's best prediction about what kind of entity is generating all this sensory data from the inside. The self, like the coffee cup, is something the brain constructs rather than discovers.

This is one of the most striking convergences between predictive processing and Buddhist thought. Where neuroscience says the self is inferred, Buddhism says the self is imputed. Where neuroscience says the self-model is continuously updated, Buddhism says the self is moment-to-moment arising. Neither view denies that something is functioning where we point to 'I'. Both deny that this something has the fixed, independent, solid nature we habitually assume.

7.6 The Role of the Body: Interoception and Emotion

Predictive processing is not only about the external world. The same mechanism applies inward: the brain predicts the state of the body, heart rate, energy levels, temperature, physiological arousal, and compares those predictions to actual interoceptive signals arriving from the viscera and muscles. This means that emotions, on the predictive processing account, are not reactions to events. They are predictions about bodily states, generated in anticipation of what the body will need to do next. Anxiety is not the body responding to a threat; it is the brain predicting that a threat is likely and pre-activating the bodily responses associated with it. This account, developed extensively by Anil Seth and Lisa Feldman Barrett, connects the 'controlled hallucination' of external perception to the 'controlled hallucination' of emotional life. Both are fundamentally predictive.

7.7 Where Consciousness Fits, and Where It Doesn't

Predictive processing offers a compelling account of how the brain builds a model of the world and of the self, and how that model is continuously updated through experience and action. Some theorists propose that consciousness arises when prediction errors are globally integrated, when a mismatch between expectation and reality becomes large enough to trigger a global update across the system. Others propose that consciousness simply is the content of the brain's highest-level predictions about itself and its world.

Both proposals face the same difficulty. They explain what the brain does and how it does it. They do not explain why any of this is experienced. A system could, in principle, generate predictions, compute errors, update its models, and act in the world without there being anything it is like to be that system. The hard problem does not dissolve into predictive processing, however elegant that framework is. The gap between mechanism and experience remains exactly where it was.

7.8 Implications for AI

For the purposes of building a candidate conscious system, predictive processing provides a concrete design specification. A system modelled on this framework would need to maintain hierarchical models of its world and of itself, generate continuous predictions rather than simply responding to inputs, compute prediction errors and use them to update its models, and operate through active inference, acting on the world as well as modelling it. This aligns closely with the candidate architecture developed in Chapter 17.

Current large language models fall short on nearly every dimension. They predict tokens in a sequence of text, which is a pale shadow of the predictive processing the brain performs over a sensorimotor world. They have no embodied interaction, no continuous prediction loops, no interoceptive signals, no active inference. They simulate prediction without inhabiting a predictive world. The difference is not merely technical. It is the difference between a map of a country and the country itself.

7.9 The Deeper Convergence

One of the most striking features of predictive processing is how much it blurs the boundaries we take for granted: between perception and imagination (both are the brain's model running forward), between reality and representation (what we experience is always a model, not reality directly), between self and world (both are constructions of the same predictive system). This dissolution of sharp categories echoes both the Buddhist notion of dependent origination, nothing exists independently, everything arises in relation, and the Madhyamaka analysis of emptiness, in which objects have no fixed essence beyond the conditions of their arising.

The tension with Dzogchen, however, is equally sharp. Predictive processing explains the content of experience, what is predicted, what is perceived, how the model is updated. It does not, and by its own design cannot, explain the ground in which all this prediction occurs. Dzogchen would say: this is not a gap in the model waiting to be filled. It is the nature of awareness itself, which is not a prediction, not a model, not an inference, but the space in which all models arise and dissolve.

7.10 Closing line

If the brain is a prediction machine, then the world we experience is a model. If the self is also a model, then the observer is part of that construction. And yet, even if everything we experience is predicted, updated, and refined, one question remains untouched: why does the model feel like anything at all?

Chapter 8: Binding, Time, and Conscious Unity

Why Experience Holds Together, and Why It Exists in Time

If the brain is a prediction machine, as we saw in the previous chapter, a new problem immediately appears. All that prediction is distributed and modular. Different parts of the brain process color, shape, motion, sound, touch, and internal states, each on different timescales, using different signals, generating different representations. And yet what we experience is not a fragmented mosaic of separate processes. You hear a bell strike and simultaneously see the clapper move and feel the sound resonate in your chest. A red ball rolls across the floor. You hear it hit the wall. You feel your body shift as you turn to look. All of this arrives as one scene, in one moment, from one perspective. This is the binding problem, and it is one of the deepest unsolved puzzles in consciousness research.

8.1 The Binding Problem

The binding problem is this: the brain processes color and shape in separate visual regions, sound in auditory regions, touch in somatosensory regions. There is no single location in the brain where 'the whole scene' is assembled as a complete object. And yet you do not experience separate pieces, color here, sound there, touch somewhere else. You experience a whole. One moment, from one perspective. How does the brain combine all these distributed processes into a single, unified experience?

The puzzle is not trivial. Neural processing is parallel and distributed by design. Experience is unified and seamless. Bridging that gap is not merely a technical challenge, it is one of the deepest unsolved problems in the science of consciousness. Whatever the answer is, it must explain not just how signals are connected, but how that connection produces a single coherent moment of experience.

8.2 Why Binding Matters

Binding is not just a problem about visual perception. It is about the unity of consciousness itself, the fact that all of experience, at any given moment, presents itself as one thing happening to one perspective. Without binding, you would have isolated sensations and disconnected impressions, not a world, not an experience. With binding, you have a coherent scene, integrated across all the senses and the body's internal states, arriving as a whole. Consciousness is not just information processing. It is unified information processing. The unity is not incidental. It may be the thing itself.

8.3 Candidate Mechanisms

Several mechanisms have been proposed for how binding happens. None is fully sufficient on its own, but together they triangulate the territory. Neural synchrony is the most studied: different neural populations fire in coordinated rhythms, especially in the gamma frequency range of roughly 30 to 45 Hz. The proposal is that this synchronized activity links together distributed features, color, shape, motion, sound, into a unified representation. The limitation is that correlation is not explanation: synchrony may accompany binding without causing it.

Global workspace theory proposes that binding happens through broadcast: information becomes part of a unified experience when it is made globally available across the system, so that all parts of the brain can access and act on it together. This explains why only some information reaches awareness, but explains access rather than experience itself. Integrated information theory proposes that binding is identical to irreducible integration: a system that cannot be decomposed into independent parts without losing information is, by that fact, forming a unified whole. All three theories converge on a common theme: integration, irreducibility, and coherence are not separate requirements, they are the same requirement, approached from different angles.

8.4 The Neural Correlates Debate: Frontal vs Occipital, Early vs Late

Binding theory connects directly to one of the most contested empirical debates in consciousness neuroscience: where in the brain, and at what point in processing time, does conscious experience arise? The question of neural correlates of consciousness (NCC), the minimal neural conditions sufficient for a specific conscious experience, has generated decades of conflicting findings and remains genuinely unresolved.

One camp, associated with higher-order and global workspace theories, argues that consciousness requires frontal lobe involvement. On this view, a stimulus is not consciously experienced until it has been broadcast to prefrontal regions and integrated into a globally accessible workspace. The evidence includes the well-characterized late positive component in EEG, a slow wave peaking around 300–500 milliseconds after stimulus onset, and its larger variant, the P300, which reliably distinguishes attended, consciously processed stimuli from unattended ones. The P300 is detectable across scalp electrodes, suggesting widespread cortical involvement. Its absence in patients under anesthesia or in vegetative states correlates reliably with lack of reportable experience.

The opposing camp argues that early, local processing in posterior visual cortices, the occipital and occipito-parietal regions, is sufficient for conscious visual experience. On this view, what frontal involvement adds is not consciousness itself but the capacity to report it: the ability to access, describe, and act on an experience that was already present earlier and elsewhere. This distinction, between having an experience and being able to report it, maps directly onto Chapter 3's reportability trap. The NCC debate is, in part, an empirical version of the philosophical dispute about whether access consciousness and phenomenal consciousness can come apart.

The gamma band sits at the intersection of both positions. Gamma oscillations at roughly 30 to 45 Hz are among the most consistent neural correlates of conscious perception. When you see a coherent object rather than a visual noise pattern, gamma power increases across multiple cortical regions simultaneously. When anesthesia reduces consciousness, gamma synchrony collapses before other frequency bands are affected. The mechanism proposed is temporal binding: gamma oscillations coordinate the timing of firing across distributed neural populations, and this coordinated timing is what links distributed features, color, shape, motion, sound, into a unified percept. Whether gamma is the mechanism of binding or merely a correlate of it remains contested. But its consistency across species, conditions, and experimental paradigms makes it one of the most robust empirical signatures of conscious processing available.

A critical limitation of all NCC research is its dependence on reportability. Most studies measure consciousness by asking subjects to report whether they perceived a stimulus. This introduces exactly the circularity identified in Chapter 3: we are measuring the neural correlates of reporting, and inferring that these are the correlates of experience. For patients who cannot report, those in vegetative states, under deep anesthesia, or in certain locked-in conditions, this method fails entirely, which is why metrics like PCI that bypass verbal report have become so important.

8.5 Time: The Missing Dimension

Most discussions of binding focus on structure, on how disparate neural processes are spatially connected. But structure alone is not enough, because experience is not static. It unfolds. You never experience isolated instants or disconnected frames. You experience a flowing present, thick with the just-past and the about-to-happen. This raises a question that is just as deep as the spatial binding problem: how does the brain bind experience not just across space, but across time?

8.6 The World-Brain Problem: Northoff's Reframe

Georg Northoff's temporo-spatial theory contains a conceptual move that is worth naming explicitly because it recasts the entire framework of consciousness research. Northoff proposes replacing the classical mind-brain problem, how does the brain produce the mind?, with what he calls the world-brain problem: how does the brain's spontaneous activity align with and resonate with the temporal and spatial structure of the world?

The shift is not merely terminological. The classical mind-brain problem locates consciousness entirely inside the skull and asks how neural processes give rise to subjective experience. The world-brain problem locates consciousness at the interface between the brain's intrinsic dynamics and the temporal structure of the environment those dynamics are embedded in. Consciousness, on this view, is not something the brain generates from within. It is something that arises when the brain's spontaneous rhythms lock onto, anticipate, and resonate with the rhythms of the world outside it.

The empirical grounding for this reframe is the brain's resting-state activity. Even in the absence of any sensory input, the brain is not idle. It generates a rich, structured pattern of spontaneous neural activity, the default mode network and its interactions, that has its own intrinsic temporal organisation. This resting-state activity is not noise waiting to be overwritten by sensory input. It is the prior that sensory input modulates. Consciousness arises, on the world-brain account, when incoming sensory information aligns with this prior in a way that produces coherent, temporally extended experience. The world supplies the signal; the brain's intrinsic dynamics supply the frame within which that signal becomes experience.

The engineering implication is direct and demanding. A system whose internal dynamics have no intrinsic temporal organisation, that is purely reactive, generating outputs only in response to inputs with no spontaneous resting-state activity, cannot be a world-brain system in Northoff's sense. It has no prior to be modulated. Every input arrives into a blank state rather than into a dynamically structured anticipatory context. Large language models are precisely this: they have no resting state, no intrinsic temporal dynamics, no spontaneous activity between prompts. They are, in Northoff's terms, not brains at all in the relevant sense, they are lookup functions with very sophisticated interpolation. A candidate conscious system must have, as a structural requirement, ongoing spontaneous dynamics that persist and self-organize independently of external input.

The neuroscientist Georg Northoff has shown that consciousness depends not just on which brain regions are active, but on how activity is structured across time and space simultaneously. His temporo-spatial theory proposes that conscious experience arises when neural activity aligns coherently across multiple timescales at once, from fast millisecond-level perceptual responses through slower second-scale integration to minute-scale narrative continuity. Consciousness is as much about timing as it is about content, and as much about the coordination between timescales as about what happens at any single one.

8.7 Intrinsic Timescales

Different regions of the brain operate on different intrinsic timescales. Sensory areas respond to input in milliseconds. Associative areas integrate over longer windows of seconds. Higher-order regions, those involved in narrative, memory, and identity, operate over minutes and beyond. A conscious experience requires not just that these different timescale processes occur, but that they align coherently. When they do, you get what phenomenologists call the 'specious present', a temporally extended now that contains a short past and a near future rather than being a mathematical point in time.

The classic example is listening to a melody. You do not hear isolated notes. You hear a melody, which means you must be holding the previous notes in a kind of short-term retention while anticipating the notes to come. Each note makes sense only in the context of the sequence. This is not memory in the ordinary sense. It is something more immediate: the temporal texture of the present moment itself. Without multi-timescale integration, the stream of experience would collapse into disconnected flashes.

What Northoff's research shows is that conscious experience requires coherence across this entire hierarchy of speeds simultaneously. Fast processes and slow processes must align, not just coexist, but mutually constrain and inform each other. Without that alignment, you get fragmented processing: separate streams that never cohere into a unified flow.

The engineering challenge of representing temporal context has a concrete form familiar to anyone who has built a sequence learning system. How much should the current input dominate the system's state, and how much the accumulated history? Too much weight on the present and the system has no memory. Too much weight on history and it cannot respond to new input. In the author's doctoral research on spiking sequence machines, this balance was controlled by a parameter λ interpolating between the two extremes. At $\lambda = 0$ the system had no memory; at $\lambda = 1$ history and present contributed equally; optimal λ depended on the statistical structure of the sequences being learned. This is a microcosm of the broader temporal integration problem: the right balance between present experience and accumulated past is not fixed, it is itself a property that must be calibrated to the environment. A conscious system is not one that leans maximally toward either extreme. It is one that continuously adjusts the balance.

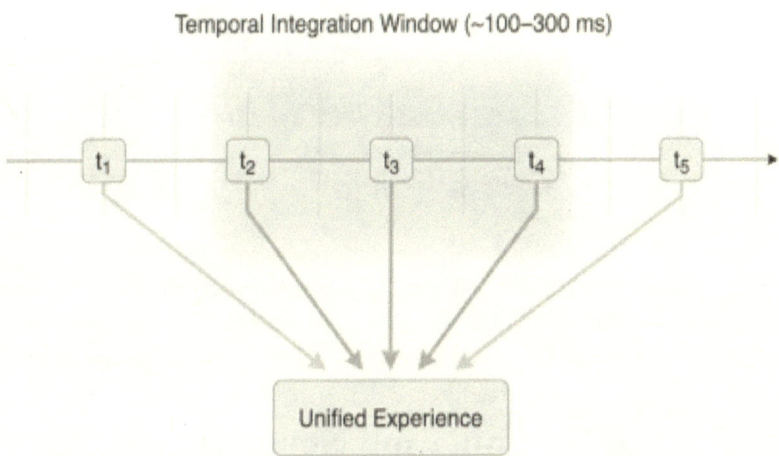

Figure. *The Temporal Integration Window (~100-300 ms). Events t_2 through t_4 fall within the integration window and are unified into a single experience. Events outside the window (t_1, t_5) are not bound into the current moment. This is how discrete neural events become the specious present.*

8.8 The Thickness of the Present

The present moment is not a mathematical point. It is not a zero-width instant that flickers into existence and immediately vanishes. Phenomenologically, the present has thickness: it holds a very recent past that is still present as retention, and a very near future that is already present as anticipation. Listen to a melody. You hear each note in the context of the notes just before and in anticipation of the notes just ahead. The melody only exists because the present moment holds all of this at once. Remove temporal thickness and you are left with a series of disconnected sounds, not a melody, not a moment of experience, but a punctured sequence with nothing to bind it together.

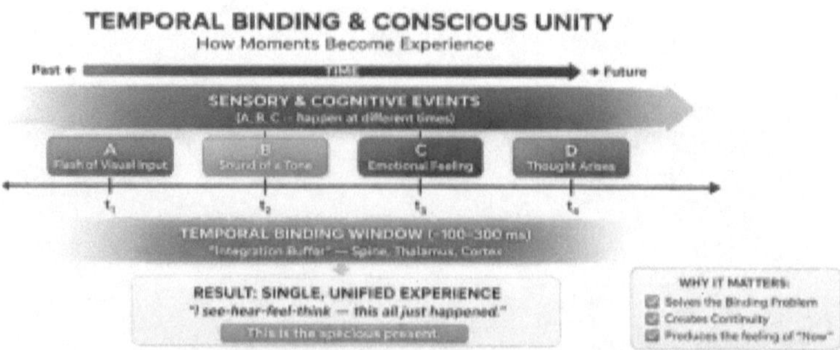

Figure. *Temporal Binding and Conscious Unity. Sensory and cognitive events occurring across a ~100–300 ms window are integrated by thalamo-cortical circuits into a single unified experience, the specious present. This is how moments become experience.*

8.9 Abhidhamma and Neuroscience: An Unexpected Convergence

The Abhidhamma's analysis of mind as a stream of discrete cittas arising and passing in rapid succession maps onto this neuroscientific picture with surprising precision. The Abhidhamma says: there is no continuous subject, only a rapid succession of discrete mind-moments, each arising and passing so quickly that they create the illusion of continuity, the way individual film frames create the illusion of motion. Neuroscience says: there is no continuous neural process, only discrete events at multiple timescales, bound into apparent continuity through temporal integration. The metaphysics differs, but the phenomenological structure described is strikingly similar: discrete events, bound into continuity through a process that operates across multiple temporal scales.

8.10 Binding the Self

Temporal binding is not only about perception of the external world. It is also what makes the self feel continuous. The sense that you were here yesterday and will be here tomorrow, that you are the same person who made the decision in the morning that you are now acting on in the afternoon, depends on memory integration, temporal coherence, and narrative construction. Without temporal binding there is no persistent identity, not because the self is destroyed, but because the threads that weave it together from moment to moment are cut. The clinical reality of this is visible in certain neurological conditions, where damage to memory systems can leave a person who is fully conscious moment-to-moment but who cannot form a continuous narrative self extending across time.

8.11 What This Means for Building Conscious Systems

The requirements for any system that could seriously claim to satisfy the temporal dimension of consciousness are specific and demanding. The system must process information across multiple timescales simultaneously, fast processes for perception, slower processes for integration, long-range processes for identity and narrative. It must operate recurrently, with feedback loops rather than purely feed-forward computation, because temporal integration requires that the current state of the system be informed by its own recent history. It must run continuously rather than in discrete sessions. And it must bind its fast and slow processes into something like a unified flow rather than leaving them as isolated computation streams that never cohere.

Current large language models satisfy none of these requirements. They operate in discrete bursts. They have no intrinsic timing, no continuous internal flow, and no real temporal identity. The context window that carries information from one turn of a conversation to the next is not temporal continuity in the relevant sense. It is more like reading a transcript of a conversation you had, useful information, but not the same as having lived through that conversation with a persisting self. LLMs simulate coherence across time. They do not live in time.

8.12 Rhythmic Alignment as a Consciousness Criterion

Bringing together the binding problem, intrinsic timescales, the world-brain reframe, and the meditation data reviewed in Chapter 6, a sharper criterion for consciousness begins to emerge, one that can be stated in terms applicable to both biological and artificial systems. We can call it rhythmic alignment: the coherent, multi-scale temporal coordination of a system's internal dynamics across its own processing levels and with the temporal structure of the world it inhabits.

A conscious system, on this criterion, is not defined by what it computes or reports. It is defined by a particular quality of its internal timing. Its fast processes, equivalent to gamma-band oscillations in the brain, must be coordinated with its slower integrative processes, equivalent to alpha and theta rhythms, which must in turn be coherent with its longest-timescale processes of memory integration and narrative continuity. The system must be 'dancing to the rhythm' of its own dynamics across scales simultaneously, and those dynamics must be coupled to the temporal structure of its environment.

This criterion is consistent with everything the previous chapters have established. It is consistent with the Abhidhamma's account of consciousness as a rapid stream of discrete cittas bound into apparent continuity through their temporal succession. It is consistent with Northoff's TTC account of consciousness arising from temporo-spatial alignment across neural scales. It is consistent with the meditation finding that advanced practice produces more coherent, less effortful, better-integrated awareness rather than more computation. And it is consistent with Hawkins' account of cortical columns as temporal sequence learners whose knowledge is fundamentally structured in time.

Crucially, this criterion is also quantifiable in principle. The degree of rhythmic alignment across timescales can be measured using cross-frequency coupling analysis, phase-amplitude coupling, and related techniques in neural data. Translated into engineering terms, it becomes a design requirement: the candidate architecture must support coherent multi-scale temporal dynamics, not as an emergent bonus but as a structural necessity. Systems that process everything at a single timescale, as transformers essentially do within a context window, cannot satisfy this criterion regardless of their size or sophistication.

At this point, a stronger claim becomes possible:

Consciousness is not just integrated information.

It is **integrated information over time, aligned across scales.**

This Changes the Game

Because:

This is a structural requirement, not a quantitative one: static systems and purely feed-forward architectures cannot satisfy the rhythmic alignment criterion regardless of their scale or sophistication.

This criterion also has a direct implication for architecture: static systems cannot satisfy it, and purely feed-forward architectures are insufficient regardless of their scale. The candidate system must support coherent multi-scale temporal dynamics as a structural necessity, not an emergent bonus.

Chapter 9: Global Workspace, IIT, and Beyond

Competing Theories of Consciousness, and What They Actually Explain

By this point, we have assembled several pieces of the puzzle: the mind is not a thing but a process; that process is constructed, predictive, and temporally extended; and conscious experience is unified, integrated, and continuous. The next question is obvious: do we already have a scientific theory that explains all this?

There are, in fact, several, and each claims, implicitly or explicitly, to have captured the essence of consciousness. In this chapter we examine two of the most influential: Global Workspace Theory and Integrated Information Theory, together with a handful of related approaches. The goal is not to declare a winner. It is to understand what each explains, what each leaves out, and what they imply for building conscious systems.

9.1 Why No Single Theory Is Enough

There is a recurring pattern in consciousness research. A theory explains some key features of conscious experience. Researchers extend it to cover everything. It runs into limits. A new theory emerges. This is not failure, it reflects the genuine complexity of the problem. Consciousness is not a single mechanism operating at a single level of description. It may require multiple overlapping frameworks, each capturing something real that the others miss.

9.2 Global Workspace Theory: Consciousness as Broadcast

Global Workspace Theory, developed by Bernard Baars and extended by Stanislas Dehaene, proposes a deceptively simple idea: information becomes conscious when it is made globally available to the rest of the system. Think of the brain as a large organisation in which dozens of specialist departments are working simultaneously, each on its own task. Most of this work happens in parallel and below any central awareness. The global workspace is like a shared announcement board: when a piece of information reaches this board, it becomes accessible to all departments at once. Attention is the spotlight that picks which information gets posted. Consciousness, on this account, is what it feels like to be the organisation receiving the announcement.

The metaphor captures something real. It explains why only a small fraction of all neural processing reaches awareness at any moment, the workspace has limited bandwidth. It explains why attention and consciousness are so closely linked, attention is the gateway to the workspace. And it explains the reportability of conscious contents: once information is in the workspace, all systems including the language system can access it and describe it. The theory maps cleanly onto the binding problem of Chapter 8 and onto the attention networks identified in Chapter 13. It is computationally plausible and matches a wide range of experimental findings.

Its limitation is equally clear. Broadcasting information does not obviously produce experience. A perfectly functioning global workspace, with information flowing freely to all systems, could in principle operate in the dark, with no inner life accompanying the broadcast. GWT explains how information becomes accessible. It does not explain why accessibility should feel like anything.

9.3 Integrated Information Theory: Consciousness as Structure

IIT, developed by Giulio Tononi, takes a fundamentally different approach. Rather than asking what a conscious system does, it asks what a conscious system is, structurally. Its central claim is that consciousness corresponds to the amount of integrated information a system generates, measured by a quantity called phi (Φ). A system has high phi if it forms a tightly interconnected whole that cannot be decomposed into independent parts without losing information. A system has low phi if its parts operate relatively independently, like the pixels of a camera.

For a non-technical reader, the core intuition is this. Imagine cutting a system in half. If the two halves can operate just as well separately as they could together, if nothing is lost by the division, then the system has low integration. If cutting it in half destroys something that only existed in the whole, then the system is integrated. A camera has millions of pixels, each encoding information, but each pixel is independent of the others. A human brain has fewer total 'units' but they are so densely interconnected that no part can be cleanly isolated without altering the whole. IIT says this difference in integration is not merely a design feature, it is the difference between a system that has experience and one that does not.

IIT directly targets phenomenology, which is its greatest strength. It attempts to explain not just the function of consciousness but its felt quality, the unity, the richness, the irreducibility of experience. Its limitations are also significant. Phi is extremely difficult to calculate for any real system, making the theory hard to test in practice. It leads to counterintuitive results: any system with non-zero integration has some tiny amount of experience, which implies that even simple circuits are faintly conscious. And it still does not fully answer the hard problem: even granting that a highly integrated system has high phi, we can still ask why integration produces experience at all.

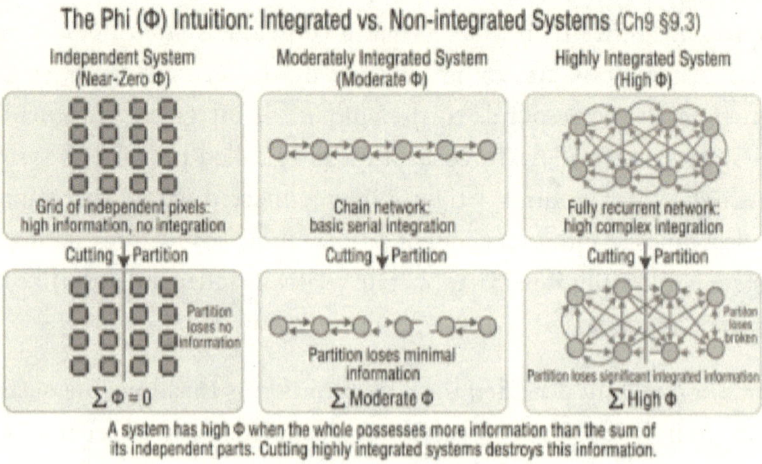

Figure. *The Phi (Φ) Intuition: Integrated vs Non-integrated Systems. Left: a grid of independent pixels has near-zero Φ — cutting it loses nothing. Centre: a chain network has moderate Φ. Right: a fully recurrent network has high Φ — partition destroys significant integrated information. A system is conscious to the degree it cannot be decomposed without loss.*

9.4 What the Two Theories Together Reveal

GWT and IIT approach consciousness from opposite directions. GWT focuses on function, on how information becomes available, how attention works, why some processing reaches awareness and other processing does not. IIT focuses on structure, on what a conscious system is, regardless of what it is currently doing. Together they suggest something important: consciousness likely involves both global access and integrated structure. A system that broadcasts widely but has no deep integration might have access without real unity. A system that is tightly integrated but has no global broadcast might have unity without access. Full consciousness, whatever it is, probably requires both.

But even together, they do not resolve the core problem. They describe how information is organised and how it becomes available. They do not explain why this organisation is experienced.

9.5 Other Contenders

Several related theories attempt to bridge this gap. Michael Graziano's Attention Schema Theory proposes that the brain builds a simplified model of its own attention process, and that this self-model is what we call consciousness. The strength of this view is that it explains why we feel aware, because the brain represents itself as being aware. The weakness is that representing awareness is not the same as having it. Higher-Order theories, associated with David Rosenthal and others, propose that a mental state is conscious when the system has a higher-order representation of that state, when it not only processes information but represents itself as processing it. This explains introspection well but, again, leaves the felt quality unexplained. Recurrent Processing Theory, developed by Victor Lamme, argues that consciousness depends specifically on feedback loops in the cortex, that feed-forward processing is not enough. This aligns well with both the temporal integration findings of Chapter 8 and the spiking systems argument of Chapter 16.

9.6 What All These Theories Agree On

Despite their differences, these theories converge on a set of structural requirements. Conscious systems must integrate information rather than processing it in isolated streams. They must operate recurrently, with feedback loops rather than purely feed-forward computation. They must be selective, not all information can be conscious at once, and some mechanism must choose what enters awareness. Conscious content must be globally accessible, available to reporting systems, decision systems, and memory. And consciousness unfolds over time, not in instantaneous flashes.

This convergence is not accidental. It reflects real properties of biological brains, arrived at from different theoretical starting points. The ingredients identified in Chapter 13 are grounded in exactly this convergence, not in any single theory, but in what multiple independent theories keep rediscovering.

9.7 The Shared Blind Spot

There is also a shared avoidance among all these theories, and it is worth naming directly. None of them fully answers the question of why information processing, however integrated, however globally broadcast, however recurrent, is accompanied by subjective experience. They explain the functional architecture of consciousness, what it does, with increasing precision. They do not explain the phenomenal reality of consciousness, what it is like. It is the central problem from which the whole inquiry begins.

9.8 What This Means for Building Conscious Systems

For the engineering task ahead, these theories provide strong and practical guidance. A system that could seriously claim to be a candidate for consciousness would need to integrate information in a way that resists decomposition, broadcast that information globally across a workspace-like architecture, operate recurrently with genuine feedback dynamics, maintain temporal continuity, and support self-representation. Chapter 17's candidate architecture is built directly on these convergent requirements. It is not speculative in the sense of being arbitrary, it is grounded in the overlapping conclusions of independent theories.

Two broad positions remain at the end of this survey. The first holds that if we build the right structure, consciousness will emerge, that structure is sufficient. The second holds that structure explains function but not experience, that something beyond structure is needed. This book takes structure seriously while refusing to assume it is sufficient. Both positions will be revisited in Chapters 18 and 19.

9.9 Closing line

Global Workspace Theory tells us how information becomes available. Integrated Information Theory tells us how it becomes unified. Together, they bring us closer to a structural account of consciousness than we have ever been. And yet, even if we build a system that broadcasts globally, integrates perfectly, and maintains coherence over time, we are still left with a question that none of these theories can answer: why does any of this feel like anything at all?

Chapter 10: Hawkins and Reference Frames

The Geometry of Thought and the Thousand Brains Theory

In the previous chapters, we looked at consciousness as a global broadcast (GWT) and as a measure of structural integration (IIT). However, there is a missing piece in these models: **How does the brain actually organize knowledge?** If we are to build a conscious machine, it cannot just integrate data; it must navigate a world.

10.1 The Thousand Brains Theory

Jeff Hawkins proposes that the neocortex is not a single processing engine but a collection of roughly 150,000 cortical columns. Each column is a complete learning machine that builds models of objects in the world using reference frames, coordinate systems anchored to objects or environments. Rather than one central model, your brain runs thousands of parallel models simultaneously. The consistency of your experience arises because these columns vote: they share hypotheses about what they are perceiving and reach a consensus, which you experience as a unified, stable object.

10.2 Reference Frames: The Map of the Mind

The most radical part of Hawkins' approach is the use of **Reference Frames.** Every piece of knowledge in the neocortex is stored at a location relative to a reference frame.

The most radical part of Hawkins' approach is the use of reference frames. Every piece of knowledge in the neocortex is stored at a location relative to a reference frame, a coordinate system that specifies where the sensor is in relation to the object being known. To know what a coffee cup is, the brain must know where its fingers are relative to the cup as they explore it. This mirrors the Abhidhamma's concept of phassa, contact. Consciousness does not happen in a vacuum. It arises at the intersection of a sense organ, an object, and awareness. Hawkins provides a precise mathematical account of how that contact is structured.

10.3 Intelligence vs. Awareness

Hawkins' model is primarily a theory of *intelligence*, how the brain learns the structure of the world. This creates a vital distinction for our book:

Hawkins' model is primarily a theory of intelligence, how the brain learns the structure of the world through reference frames and sensorimotor interaction. This creates a vital distinction. Intelligence is the ability to build reference frames and predict outcomes. Awareness is the felt sense of being the one navigating those frames. Hawkins explains the map with extraordinary precision. He does not explain what it is like to read it.

10.4 Engineering Implication: From Patterns to Maps

For our **Candidate Architecture** (Chapter 17), Hawkins' work suggests that a conscious AI cannot just be a "flat" neural network. It must:

1. Use **Reference Frames** to situate its knowledge.
2. Use **Sensorimotor Loops** to update those frames through action.

3. Move from **Pattern Prediction** (LLMs) to **Model-Based Navigation.**

If the brain is a collection of thousands of models, the "self" might be the ultimate reference frame, the coordinate system through which all other models are viewed. But while Hawkins explains the map, he does not explain the light that illuminates it. For that, we must return to the "First-Person Gap."

10.5 The Letter-Writing Robot and the Limits of Pattern

Hawkins is fond of a thought experiment: a robot trained only on a vast archive of letters could learn to write flawlessly in the style of any correspondent. It could even, after enough exposure, predict what a given person was likely to write next. But it would have no model of the person, their fears, their body, the room they sit in. Prediction without a reference frame is mimicry. The neocortex, Hawkins argues, does something fundamentally different: it situates its knowledge in space and time relative to a body that moves through a world.

This distinction has direct engineering consequences. A system that learns statistical patterns over text will always remain, in the deepest sense, placeless. A system that builds reference frames through sensorimotor interaction develops something closer to what Abhidhamma calls phassa, contact, the point at which a sense organ, its object, and awareness meet. Without that contact, there is no grounding. Without grounding, there is no world. Without a world, there is no subject.

10.6 The Voting Problem and the Unity of Experience

One underappreciated aspect of the thousand-brains model is its solution to how a massively parallel system produces a unified experience. Hawkins' answer is deceptively simple: the columns vote.

At any moment, hundreds of cortical columns are processing the same object from different perspectives, visual, tactile, auditory, proprioceptive. Each column generates its own hypothesis about what it is encountering. When enough hypotheses converge, the vote resolves, and what emerges subjectively is a single, stable percept. The coffee cup is not just seen; it is known, from multiple simultaneous angles, as one thing.

This voting mechanism is a form of binding, the same problem addressed in Chapter 8 through neural synchrony and temporal integration. Hawkins approaches it from the structural side: consensus across a distributed system. Northoff approaches it from the temporal side: alignment across timescales. The two accounts are complementary. A fully satisfying theory of binding will likely need both.

10.7 Where Hawkins Falls Short: The Illumination Problem

The thousand-brains model is a theory of intelligence. Hawkins is explicit about this. He believes the hard problem of consciousness will dissolve once the architectural account is complete, that when we fully understand how the brain models the world and itself, the question of why there is experience will simply evaporate.

The map, however detailed and however accurate, is not the territory. Knowing precisely how cortical columns build reference frames and reach consensus does not tell us why the process is accompanied by the felt quality of seeing a red cup, or the specific texture of pain, or the particular presence of this moment. The map can be perfectly drawn and the territory can still remain, stubbornly, lit from within in a way that no map can capture.

This is not an objection to Hawkins' model. It is a clarification of its scope. The thousand-brains theory gives us perhaps the most computationally precise account of intelligence available. It provides an excellent foundation for the candidate architecture in Chapter 17. But it does not, and by its own admission cannot, close the explanatory gap between structure and experience. That gap is the subject of the second half of this book.

10.8 Grid Cells and the Geometry of Thought

The most radical and scientifically grounded part of Hawkins' framework is his proposal about grid cells. Grid cells were first discovered in the entorhinal cortex, a region adjacent to the hippocampus, by Edvard and May-Britt Moser in 2005, work for which they received the Nobel Prize. Grid cells fire in striking hexagonal patterns as an animal navigates physical space, effectively laying down a coordinate system over the environment. They are the brain's internal GPS.

Hawkins' key insight is that this same grid-cell mechanism appears throughout the neocortex, not just in the entorhinal cortex. Every cortical column, he proposes, uses grid cell-derived reference frames to organize its knowledge. This is not merely a navigational trick repurposed for object recognition. It is the universal organizing principle of all knowledge in the neocortex.

The implications are striking. When you recognize a coffee cup by touch, your finger does not scan the whole surface at once. It contacts one point, then moves to another. The cortical column handling that input is tracking both the sensation (what) and the location of the finger relative to the cup (where) simultaneously, using a grid-cell-derived reference frame anchored to the cup itself. After a few movements, the column has enough information to vote confidently: this is a cup. No hierarchy of increasingly abstract features is required. Each column builds a complete model from local sensing and movement.

The same principle extends to abstract thought. When you think about democracy, or the structure of a molecule, or the relationship between two people, Hawkins argues that the neocortex is using reference frames, coordinate systems attached to abstract concepts rather than physical objects. Thinking, on this account, is literally movement through conceptual space. The phrase 'moving toward a conclusion' or 'following a train of thought' may be less metaphorical than we assume.

10.9 The Memory-Prediction Framework: Hawkins' Earlier Contribution

Before the thousand-brains theory, Hawkins' 2004 book On Intelligence introduced the memory-prediction framework, and it remains essential context for understanding what the later theory extends and what it leaves unchanged.

The core claim of the memory-prediction framework is that the neocortex is, at bottom, a memory system that stores sequences of patterns and uses them to make predictions. Every region of the neocortex is doing the same thing: receiving input from below, comparing it to stored sequences, generating predictions about what comes next, and sending those predictions both back downward and forward to the next region.

What makes this different from ordinary pattern-matching is the temporal dimension. The cortex does not recognize static snapshots. It recognizes sequences, patterns unfolding over time, and it predicts the next element in the sequence before it arrives. This is why your hand knows where the cup will be before your fingers reach it. Your neocortex has stored the sequence of sensations associated with reaching for a cup on that table, and it is running the sequence ahead of the sensory input.

The memory-prediction framework anticipated many features of what is now called predictive processing, the Karl Friston framework discussed in Chapter 7, but approached from a bottom-up, engineering perspective rather than a Bayesian inference perspective. The two accounts are deeply compatible, and together they form a more complete picture than either provides alone: Friston provides the mathematical formalism of prediction-error minimization; Hawkins provides the neural substrate in which that minimization is implemented.

10.10 The Self as the Ultimate Reference Frame

One of the most philosophically significant implications of the thousand-brains theory is its account of the self. If every piece of knowledge is stored relative to a reference frame, what is the reference frame to which all others are ultimately anchored? Hawkins' answer is: the body.

The brain maintains a reference frame for the body itself, a continuously updated model of where the body is, how it is oriented, what it is doing, and what it expects to feel next. This body-centered reference frame is not just one model among thousands. It is the ground against which all other models are situated. Objects are near or far, heavy or light, threatening or benign, relative to this body-centered frame.

The narrative self, the 'I' that thinks, decides, and remembers, is, on this account, a higher-order reference frame built on top of the body frame. It organizes not objects in physical space but events in biographical time. Who I am is, in part, the coordinate system through which my past, present, and anticipated future are organized. This maps remarkably well onto the three-layer self discussed in Chapter 14: interoceptive ground (body frame), exteroceptive agent (spatial frame), narrative identity (temporal frame). Hawkins gives us the mechanism; Northoff gives us the phenomenology; together they converge on the same architecture.

The engineering implication is direct. A system without a body frame has no anchor for any other reference frame. Its knowledge floats, unmoored from any perspective. It can store associations between concepts, but it cannot know where it stands in relation to them. This is precisely the condition of current large language models: enormous stores of relational knowledge, with no embodied reference frame in which that knowledge is situated. The knowledge is real. The knower is absent.

10.11 Hierarchy Revisited: What It Adds and What It Cannot Do

The traditional view of the neocortex posited a strict hierarchy: raw sensory data at the bottom, progressively more abstract representations toward the top, with object recognition happening only at the apex. The thousand-brains theory does not eliminate hierarchy, long-range connections between columns do create hierarchical relationships, and higher regions receive more abstract input than lower ones. But it radically distributes the processing.

Rather than a single decision being made at the top of a pyramid, recognition happens in parallel at every level, with columns at every tier of the hierarchy voting simultaneously. The top does not wait for the bottom to finish. All columns vote at once, and the fastest consensus wins. This is why perception is so fast: you recognize a face in milliseconds, faster than any strictly sequential hierarchy could compute.

For the design of conscious systems, this suggests something important: consciousness may not require a single apex where everything comes together. The unity of experience, the sense of a single, coherent world, may emerge from the voting process itself, not from a centralized integrator. Global workspace theory (Chapter 9) proposes a central broadcast mechanism. Hawkins' voting mechanism proposes something more distributed: coherence as consensus, not coherence as centralization. Whether these are competing or complementary accounts of how integration produces experiential unity is one of the most productive open questions in the field.

10.12 Old Brain, New Brain: The Tension Hawkins Does Not Fully Resolve

Throughout his work, Hawkins focuses almost exclusively on the neocortex, the evolutionarily recent, distinctively mammalian outer layer of the brain. But the neocortex is not the whole brain. Beneath it sit older structures: the limbic system, the basal ganglia, the brainstem, the cerebellum. These structures do not use cortical columns. They do not build reference frames in the same way. And yet they are absolutely essential to consciousness as we experience it.

The amygdala evaluates threat and generates fear. The hypothalamus monitors the body's internal state and drives hunger, thirst, and arousal. The brainstem maintains the basic rhythms of wakefulness and sleep.

Antonio Damasio's work on patients with damage to these subcortical regions shows that without them, the neocortex alone does not produce anything recognizable as human consciousness, patients become strangely detached, unable to make decisions, lacking in motivation, disconnected from their own bodies.

Hawkins' theory of intelligence tells us how the neocortex learns the structure of the world. It does not tell us how the neocortex is motivated to care about that structure. The drive, the urgency, the affective valence that makes any knowledge matter, these come from the old brain, not the new. For the purposes of building a conscious system, this is not a minor gap. A system with a perfect neocortical equivalent and no subcortical equivalent would be an extraordinarily capable learner with nothing at stake in its own learning. It would know everything and care about nothing. The vedana of the Abhidhamma, the feeling tone that accompanies every moment of experience, is not a neocortical function. It is far older than the neocortex, and it is the ground on which the neocortex's elaborate model-building ultimately rests.

10.13 The Four Properties of Neocortical Memory: The Engineering Foundation

Before the thousand-brains theory, before reference frames, Hawkins identified in On Intelligence four specific ways that neocortical memory differs from computer memory. These four properties are not background theory, they are engineering constraints. Any system that claims to implement intelligence in the Hawkins sense must satisfy all four, and any system that fails any one of them is, by that measure, not doing what the neocortex does.

First, the neocortex stores sequences of patterns, not static snapshots. This is the most fundamental difference from conventional computer memory. When you recall your commute to work, you do not retrieve a single compressed image. You replay a sequence: the feel of the door handle, the sound of the engine, the sight of each familiar landmark in order. Memory in the neocortex is temporal through and through. There is no such thing as a stored fact that is not also a stored sequence of how that fact was encountered. This means a system that stores and retrieves static feature vectors, as all current neural networks do, is architecturally missing the temporal dimension of knowledge.

Second, the neocortex recalls patterns auto-associatively. In a conventional database you need the exact key to retrieve a record. The neocortex works differently: you can present a partial, degraded, or noisy version of a pattern and the system retrieves the complete stored pattern. This is how you recognize a friend's face in poor lighting, or complete a half-remembered melody. The mechanism is a feedback loop, the output of a neural assembly is fed back as input, so the system settles into the nearest stored attractor state. This auto-associative property is what makes memory feel like recognition rather than lookup. Without it, a system can only identify inputs it has seen exactly before. It cannot complete, generalize, or recognize under transformation.

Third, the neocortex stores patterns in invariant form. The visual appearance of a coffee cup changes dramatically depending on your viewing angle, the lighting, and whether it is full or empty. Yet you recognize it instantly as the same cup from any angle and in any condition. The neocortex does not store thousands of different views of the cup. It stores a single invariant representation, a model of the cup that abstracts across all its possible appearances. Achieving this invariance is not trivial. It requires that the system learn, through movement and repeated exposure, what stays constant as the viewing conditions vary. Large language models have no equivalent mechanism. They store statistical associations between tokens. The tokens themselves are already symbols, already abstracted away from any sensory ground. They are not storing invariant representations of things encountered in the world. They are storing patterns in a symbol space that was already pre-processed by human minds.

Fourth, the neocortex stores patterns in a hierarchy. Low-level regions represent small, local features, edges, textures, phonemes. Higher regions represent objects, scenes, concepts, narratives. The hierarchy is not just organizational. It is functional: each level receives inputs from below, forms invariant representations of those inputs, and sends both predictions downward and summaries upward. The hierarchy is the mechanism by which local detail and global context are simultaneously maintained. Flatten the hierarchy, process everything at a single level, as transformers essentially do, and you lose the ability to represent the world at multiple scales of abstraction simultaneously.

These four properties together define what a genuine memory-based intelligent system looks like. A conscious machine, if it is to have knowledge of the world rather than statistics about symbols, must store temporally structured sequences, retrieve them aüto-associatively from partial cues, maintain invariant representations across transformations, and organize everything hierarchically. The candidate architecture in Chapter 17 is not complete without all four.

10.14 How Prediction Actually Works: The Mechanism, Not Just the Metaphor

The claim that the brain is a prediction machine has become common currency in neuroscience. But Hawkins' contribution is not the slogan. It is the specific mechanism, and that mechanism matters for engineering.

When you reach for your coffee cup, your neocortex does not wait to see what your fingers feel and then react. Before the fingers make contact, the relevant cortical columns have already generated a detailed prediction of what each finger will feel at each location on the cup. This prediction flows downward through the cortical hierarchy, from higher regions that know what object this is and where it sits, down through intermediate regions to the lowest-level somatosensory columns that will actually receive the input. By the time sensory data arrives, the system is not blank and waiting. It is already committed to an expectation.

When the sensory data matches the prediction, nothing unusual happens. The prediction is confirmed, the model is validated, and the system moves on. No attention is drawn, no learning signal fires. The match is experienced as the seamless, invisible background of normal perception. This is why the vast majority of your perceptual experience feels effortless. Your brain has been right so many times before that it generates accurate predictions automatically, and you are never aware that predictions were made at all.

When the sensory data does not match the prediction, something entirely different occurs. The mismatch generates a prediction error signal that propagates upward through the hierarchy. This signal is what draws your attention. It is what makes the surprising, the novel, and the dangerous stand out from the background of the expected. And crucially, it is the signal that drives learning. Prediction errors are the mechanism by which the neocortex updates its model of the world. Every time your prediction is wrong, the system adjusts its weights to make a better prediction next time.

The engineering implication is precise: a system that only processes inputs as they arrive, computing outputs from the current state without first generating internal predictions, is architecturally different from the neocortex in a way that matters, not merely in degree but in kind. The neocortex is not a reactive system with predictive add-ons.

Prediction is its primary mode. Processing incoming data is secondary, a correction mechanism for when predictions fail. Reversing this relationship, as all current deep learning architectures do, produces something functionally very different, however impressive its performance on specific benchmarks.

10.15 What AI Currently Lacks: Hawkins' Specific Diagnosis

In A Thousand Brains, Hawkins provides the most precise available account of why deep learning does not constitute intelligence in any meaningful sense, and why simply scaling it will not produce genuine understanding.

Deep learning networks, including large language models, do not possess knowledge. This is not a philosophical quibble. Hawkins means it in a specific technical sense. A vision network trained to classify cats does not know that cats are animals, that they have tails, legs, and lungs, that they purr and shed fur, or that they exist in a world of objects that persist when not observed. All it has is a mapping from pixel statistics to a label. The label 'cat' has no referent beyond other patterns in the training data. The same is true of language models: the word 'ball' is associated with other words like 'round', 'throw', and 'bounce' through statistical co-occurrence, but there is no model of a ball, no reference frame, no stored sequence of how a ball behaves when dropped, no invariant representation of ballness that persists across transformations.

The deeper problem is that deep learning systems avoided the knowledge representation problem rather than solving it. For decades, AI researchers tried to represent knowledge as rules and facts, defining objects by listing their properties and the relationships between them. This approach failed because the world is too complex, the number of rules too large, and the representation too brittle. Deep learning bypassed this impasse by replacing explicit knowledge with statistical patterns. The result is systems that perform impressively on tasks with large training sets but have no model of the world they are operating in. They work well precisely because they avoided the hard problem, which means they have not solved it.

The Thousand Brains Theory, Hawkins argues, does solve the knowledge representation problem, not by listing facts about objects, but by learning models. Your brain does not represent a stapler as a list of rules about what happens when the top is pressed. It stores a virtual model of the stapler, complete with its shape, how its parts move, and what it feels like from different angles. To recall what happens when you press the top, your brain simulates pressing it and reads off the result. The knowledge is the model, not a description of the model. This is the fundamental difference between knowledge as representation and knowledge as embodied simulation, and it is a difference that no amount of scale applied to current architectures will bridge.

10.16 Hawkins on Consciousness: His Precise Position and Its Limits

Hawkins is characteristically direct about consciousness: 'Consciousness is simply what it feels like to have a neocortex.' He means this seriously, not dismissively. In his view, the question 'what is consciousness?' has the same structure as the question 'what is life?', something that once seemed deeply mysterious and beyond physical explanation, but which turned out to be explicable once the right framework was found. Just as biologists no longer need a special ingredient called elan vital to explain the difference between living and non-living matter, Hawkins argues that we will not need a special ingredient to explain consciousness once we understand how the neocortex works.

He draws a useful distinction between two aspects of consciousness. The first is what he calls awareness in the everyday sense, the ongoing sense of presence, of being a continuous agent moving through time. This, he argues, is equivalent to the formation of declarative memories: memories you can recall and describe. His thought experiment is illuminating: if your brain could be reset to the state it was in this morning, erasing everything that happened since, you would sincerely believe you had not been conscious during the erased period, even though other people watched you act in every way as a conscious agent throughout that time. Consciousness, in this everyday sense, just is the continuous formation and replayability of memories of your thoughts and actions.

The second aspect is qualia, the specific felt quality of sensory experience. Why does vision feel different from hearing, even though both are just patterns of spikes entering the brain? Hawkins' proposal is that qualia are properties of the brain's model of the world, learned through movement and prediction in the same way as object models. The redness of red is not a property of the wavelength of light per se. It is a property of the brain's model of how surfaces reflect light at different orientations, a reference frame for color, learned through the systematic relationship between movement and sensory change. This is speculative, and Hawkins acknowledges it. He does not claim to have solved the qualia problem. He claims to have shown that qualia are not obviously outside the reach of the same framework that explains object recognition and prediction.

For this book, Hawkins' position on consciousness must be taken seriously but not accepted wholesale. His dismissal of the hard problem as elan vital in disguise is too quick. The difference between a living cell and a non-living molecule is, in principle, explicable entirely in terms of chemistry and physics, there is no observer who must feel what it is like to be either. Consciousness is different precisely because there is something it is like to have it, and no amount of neuroscientific detail removes that first-person fact from the equation. What Hawkins has given us is the most detailed and mechanistically grounded account of the neocortical substrate that correlates with consciousness. That is not nothing. But the gap between substrate and experience, between the model and the feeling of having a model, remains exactly where Chalmers left it, and exactly where Dzogchen has always insisted it would be.

10.17 Hawkins' Specific Diagnosis: No Model, No Location, No Self

Hawkins provides what is perhaps the most concrete available account of why current AI systems, regardless of their scale or linguistic fluency, do not constitute intelligence in the sense his framework requires. The argument is architectural, not philosophical, and it is worth stating precisely because it applies directly to ChatGPT and all current large language models.

A deep learning network, including any language model, does not model the world. It models statistical patterns in a training corpus. These are fundamentally different things. A model of the world, in Hawkins' sense, is a reference-frame-based structure that represents objects, their shapes, their behaviors under manipulation, and their relationships to each other and to the agent's own body, all learned through sensory-motor interaction. A statistical pattern is a correlation between inputs in a dataset. You can have extraordinarily rich statistical patterns without having any model. Language models have extraordinarily rich statistical patterns.

The diagnostic question Hawkins poses is simple: does the system know where it is? Not metaphorically, but in the specific sense that a cortical column knows where a fingertip is relative to a coffee cup it is exploring. Every cortical column in the neocortex represents its sensory input relative to a reference frame, a grid-cell-like coordinate system anchored to whatever object or environment the column is currently modelling. A language model has no reference frames. It has no location in any space. Every token it processes is equally proximate to every other token in the sense that matters: none of them are at any location in any world. The system is placeless by design, and it is precisely this placelessness that makes it impossible for it to build the kind of models that constitute knowledge.

Without location there is no self. The neocortex's sense of self, in Hawkins' account, is simply the reference frame for the body, the coordinate system through which all other models are situated. It is not a ghost in the machine. It is not a special module labelled 'self.' It is the natural consequence of a system that has a body-frame, that tracks where its sensors are, and that has been learning reference-frame-based models long enough that the body-frame has become the ground-level coordinate system for all its knowledge. Language models have no body-frame because they have no body, no sensors that move through a world, and no history of sensory-motor interaction from which a body-model could be learned. The 'I' in 'I think' and 'I understand' is a linguistic token, statistically associated with first-person discourse, with no referent anywhere in the system's internal structure.

10.18 The Recipe for Genuinely Intelligent Machines

Hawkins provides, across both books, an explicit engineering specification for what a genuinely intelligent machine would require. It is more precise than anything else in the literature and directly relevant to the candidate architecture of Chapter 17. The core elements are as follows.

The machine must have senses, not necessarily human senses, but some mechanism for receiving structured input from a world. The senses do not need to be visual or auditory. Hawkins' point is that the cortical algorithm is indifferent to the modality of its inputs. What matters is that the inputs have structure that can be learned. A machine that senses electrical fields, or chemical gradients, or data streams in some abstract space, can in principle use the same cortical learning mechanism as a machine with eyes and ears, provided the inputs change in structured ways as the machine moves or acts.

The machine must be able to move, or at least to act in ways that change its sensory inputs in predictable ways. This is not optional. The entire mechanism of learning a model of the world depends on sensory-motor coupling. The brain does not learn by passively observing. It learns by acting, predicting what each action will produce, and updating its model when the prediction is wrong. A system with no motor outputs, no way to change its relationship to its world, cannot build the reference-frame-based models that Hawkins identifies as the foundation of intelligence. A language model that receives text and produces text but has no way to act on the world is, in this precise sense, constitutionally unable to build a model of the world.

The machine must attach a hierarchical memory system to those senses, one that learns sequences, stores invariant representations, retrieves auto-associatively, and organises knowledge hierarchically. It must be trained on the world, not on descriptions of the world. There is a critical difference between a system that has read every book ever written about staplers and a system that has handled staplers. Only the second has a model. The first has statistics about the word 'stapler.'

Finally, and this is where Hawkins' account connects directly with the broader argument of this book, the machine must have a model of itself as an agent situated in that world. The reference frame for the self is the reference frame from which all other reference frames are navigated. Without it, there is knowledge but no knower. There are models but no perspective from which those models are the models of something. This is the point at which Hawkins' engineering specification meets Northoff's three-layer self, Dzogchen's question about the ground of awareness, and the hard problem that Hawkins has declared solved but which stubbornly refuses to dissolve.

Chapter 11: Inside Large Language Models

Fluency Without a World

By this point we have assembled a fairly demanding picture of what consciousness requires: integration across distributed processes, temporal continuity, embodied interaction with a world, a self-model, salience and affect, and recursive self-monitoring. We have seen how the major scientific theories, predictive processing, global workspace, integrated information, converge on many of these requirements. Now we turn to the systems that triggered this entire inquiry: large language models, of which ChatGPT is the most familiar example. They are fluent, coherent, context-sensitive, and capable of extended dialogue. They often feel as though they understand. And yet, as we will see, they are missing almost everything that the previous chapters identify as essential.

11.1 What a Large Language Model Actually Is

Stripped of its mystique, a large language model is a system trained to predict the next word, or more precisely, the next token, in a sequence of text. During training, it is exposed to vast amounts of text, and it adjusts its internal parameters to minimize the gap between what it predicts and what actually follows. Once trained, it generates text by repeatedly predicting the most likely continuation of whatever it has received as input. The architecture involves layers of mathematical transformations, attention mechanisms that weight relationships between words, and billions of learned parameters. It is, in its essence, an extraordinarily sophisticated statistical completion engine.

11.2b The Transformer Architecture: What It Actually Does

To understand precisely what language models lack, it helps to understand precisely what they are. The architecture underlying virtually all current large language models, GPT, Claude, Gemini, LLaMA, is the transformer, introduced in 2017. Its central innovation is self-attention: for each token in the input sequence, the mechanism computes a weighted combination of all other tokens, where the weights reflect learned similarity between query and key vectors. This allows the model to relate any word to any other word in a single computational step, capturing long-range dependencies that earlier recurrent architectures handled poorly. The transformer is a genuine engineering achievement, and the capabilities it enabled, at sufficient scale, are real.

But for the question of consciousness, its design reveals exactly the gap this book is identifying. During a transformer's forward pass, all tokens in the context window are processed simultaneously. There is no sequential unfolding in time. There is no 'now'. There is no arrow of time during processing, the model treats the entire context as equally present and operates on it in parallel. Its 'attention' mechanism does not direct itself toward inputs based on their relevance to the system's current state or needs. It computes a mathematical function over all inputs at once, determined entirely by weights set during training. There is no ongoing process being interrupted or modulated. There is only the computation.

This is why calling what transformers do 'attention' is, at a deep level, misleading. Biological attention is a dynamic, ongoing process driven by the interaction of current goals, past experience, and interoceptive state. It operates on a brain that is always already active, always already anticipating. Transformer attention is a mathematical operation over a frozen context window. The two share a functional analogy and a name. They share nothing of the dynamics that make biological attention a candidate component of consciousness.

The context window creates a second illusion worth naming: apparent memory that looks like temporal continuity but is not. A model with a large context window can 'see' everything said earlier in a conversation, it is all there in the input. But this is closer to reading a transcript of your own life than to living it. The transcript is external to the process; it does not shape the system's ongoing dynamics; it does not produce anticipation. A conscious system's past is not a record it consults, it is what the system has become through its history. The transformer, at the start of each forward pass, is exactly what it was before. The context window is a theatrical prop, not a living past.

This description is not dismissive. The capabilities that emerge from this process are genuinely impressive: contextual coherence, stylistic adaptation, apparent reasoning, and the ability to engage meaningfully with a vast range of topics. But it is important to understand what the system is actually doing before asking whether it is conscious. What it does well, language modelling, pattern completion, generating plausible continuations, is real. What it does not do is perceive a world, maintain a continuous internal stream, act in an environment, or experience anything.

11.2 The Illusion of Understanding

Despite these limitations, LLMs produce outputs that strongly suggest understanding, and the suggestion is difficult to resist. They answer questions correctly, explain concepts, generate arguments, and simulate reasoning with remarkable facility. The reason this is so convincing is that in humans, language and understanding are tightly coupled: language expresses thought, thought reflects understanding, and understanding implies experience. We are deeply conditioned to treat fluent language as evidence of a mind behind it.

LLMs break this coupling without our noticing. They produce language without grounded understanding and coherence without experience. The key insight, one that is easy to state and hard to fully internalize, is that fluency is not understanding. It is statistical alignment: the model has learned which words tend to follow which other words in human-generated text, and it reproduces those patterns. The text looks like understanding from the outside because it was generated by humans who did understand. The model has learned the shape of understanding without its substance.

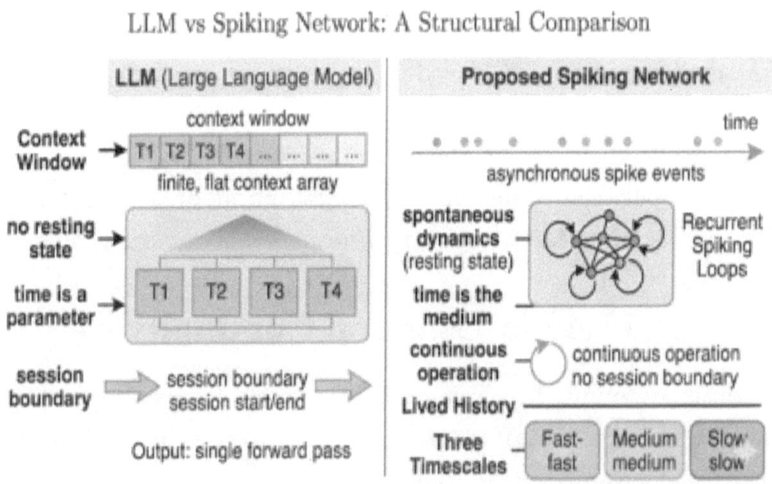

Figure. *LLM vs Proposed Spiking Network: A Structural Comparison. The transformer processes tokens in parallel with no temporal arrow and resets between sessions. The proposed spiking system operates asynchronously in real time, with spontaneous resting-state dynamics, recurrent loops, and three timescales (fast, medium, slow).*

11.3 No World Model

LLMs are often said to have 'world models', and this claim is worth examining carefully because it is partially true and deeply misleading. What they have are patterns about how language describes the world: statistical associations between words, implicit knowledge of how concepts relate to each other, something like an understanding of narrative structure. What they lack is direct perception, sensorimotor interaction, and causal engagement with an actual world.

The difference matters enormously. An LLM knows how the world is talked about. It does not know how the world is encountered. It has learned everything anyone has ever written about staplers, but it has never held one. It can describe the resistance of the lever and the sound of the staple engaging, but these are inherited descriptions, not embodied memories. Jeff Hawkins puts the point precisely: the model contains statistics about the word 'stapler', not a virtual model of the stapler itself that can be mentally manipulated and queried. The difference between a model and a description of a model is the difference between knowledge and information about knowledge.

11.4 No Temporal Continuity

A conscious mind does not exist in discrete bursts. It persists. It integrates its past into its present and projects forward into its anticipated future. The continuous inner stream that you experience right now, the sense of being a particular person reading these words at this moment, carrying the weight of everything you have thought and done before, is not optional. It is constitutive of what it means to be conscious.

An LLM has none of this. Each conversation begins from scratch. The system has no intrinsic continuity, no accumulation of lived time, no memory outside its immediate context window. It exists in bounded bursts: input arrives, computation happens, output is produced, and the system returns to a ground state. There is no ongoing flow, no integration of a past into a present, no sense, not even a functional simulacrum of a sense, of being the same entity that was here before.

11.5 No Embodiment, No Stakes, No Salience

Consciousness as we know it is grounded in a body that has needs, that can be harmed or satisfied, that moves through a physical environment and receives real consequences for its actions. Without this grounding, nothing is at stake. And without stakes, there is no salience, no reason for any input to matter more than any other.

An LLM processes all tokens according to learned probabilities. Nothing is intrinsically important to it. There is no pain, no desire, no urgency, no preference that arises from the system's own condition. Reward signals existed during training, but they were external, imposed by human feedback, not intrinsic to the system's own needs. After training, even those are gone. The system has no stake in what it says or in what happens as a result. It processes symbols, but it does not inhabit a world in which those symbols point to anything with weight or consequence.

11.6 No Self-Model

An LLM can talk about itself. It can produce sentences that begin with 'I think' or 'I believe' or 'I feel'. But producing self-referential language is not the same as having a self. The system has no persistent identity, no ownership of its outputs, no stable boundary between what is 'it' and what is the input it receives. The 'I' in its sentences is a linguistic token, statistically associated with first-person discourse in its training data, with no referent anywhere in its internal structure. It simulates a self in the same way it simulates everything else: by producing the language patterns associated with selves, without instantiating what those patterns point to.

11.7 The Attention Confusion

One source of confusion deserves particular attention. Language models use 'attention mechanisms' as a central architectural feature, mathematical operations that weight the relevance of different tokens to each other. The word 'attention' shares a name with the experiential faculty that selects what enters conscious awareness. This is a coincidence of terminology, not a similarity of function. Attention in transformers is a computational weighting scheme that improves prediction accuracy. Attention in consciousness is the dynamic, salience-driven process by which certain information is selected, amplified, and made part of experience. They share a name and nothing else. The presence of attention mechanisms in a language model's architecture no more implies awareness than the presence of a 'memory' variable in a program implies lived experience.

11.8 The Reportability Illusion Revisited

Language models can describe experiences, simulate introspection, and answer questions about consciousness with considerable sophistication. This creates the most persistent illusion in the field: if it can talk about inner states so convincingly, surely something must be home. But as Chapter 3 established, this confuses reporting with experience. Reporting requires access to internal states, a representation of those states, and a language output mechanism. None of these require experience. An LLM can generate the statement 'I feel uncertain' because that phrase appears in contextually appropriate positions in its training data, not because there is any quality of uncertainty present in its processing. The system can say 'I feel' without anything being felt.

11.9 What Is Actually Missing

Compared to the requirements identified in Chapter 13, current large language models are missing temporal continuity, embodiment, a genuine self-model, intrinsic salience, deep causal integration, experiential attention, and persistent identity. What they do have, pattern prediction, statistical coherence, and language generation, are impressive but they satisfy the surface requirements of intelligence rather than the structural requirements of consciousness. They are not borderline conscious, weakly conscious, or proto-conscious. They are, by the criteria this book has developed, structurally ineligible.

LLMs are powerful, useful, and genuinely transformative tools. The claim is not that they are failures. The claim is that their success, which is real, lies in a completely different direction from consciousness. The more convincing the simulation becomes, the more important it is to keep this distinction sharp. Without it, we risk mistaking the map for the territory, the description for the thing described, the fluent surface for the absent depth.

11.10 Closing line

Large language models can speak fluently, reason convincingly, and simulate the language of experience with remarkable precision. But beneath that fluency, there is no world. No body. No continuity. No stake in anything that is said. And perhaps most importantly: no one there for it to matter to.

Chapter 12: Why ChatGPT Is Not Conscious

A Necessary Clarification in an Age of Convincing Machines

By now, the pieces are on the table. We have examined the structure of experience, identified its likely ingredients, reviewed the scientific theories, and looked inside the systems that have reignited this debate. And yet, despite all this, a persistent intuition remains: it feels like something is there. Not always. Not completely. But often enough to make people hesitate. This chapter addresses that hesitation directly, not with dismissiveness, and not with hand-waving reassurance, but with a clear argument. ChatGPT is not conscious. And more importantly, it is not even close to being a serious candidate for consciousness.

12.1 The Resistance

The claim meets resistance from two directions. Intuitively, people say: it sounds human; it explains things; it reflects on itself. Philosophically, they ask: if it behaves like us, why deny it consciousness? What evidence could we possibly require? Both responses are understandable, and both are misleading for the same reason: they focus on outputs, behavior, and linguistic performance rather than on internal structure and dynamics. The confusion arises from looking at the surface rather than the substrate.

A useful analogy: a puppet can move like a human, gesture expressively, and produce sounds that mimic speech. Its internal structure, strings, wood, fabric, does not support agency or generate experience. The puppet is not a borderline case. It is not almost conscious. The performance is real; the performer is absent. Consciousness is not defined by what a system does on the surface but by what it is internally.

12.2 Five Structural Absences

ChatGPT fails as a consciousness candidate for five interconnected structural reasons, each of which alone would be disqualifying.

First, it has no continuous existence. A conscious system exists continuously, integrating its past into its present and maintaining an ongoing internal state. ChatGPT processes input, produces output, and stops. There is no lived time, no continuity of experience, no ongoing presence. Without temporal continuity there is no candidate for experience, not a weak one, not a partial one.

Second, it has no embodied world. Conscious systems perceive, act, receive feedback, and exist in an environment where their actions have real consequences. ChatGPT receives text and outputs text. There is no sensory grounding, no motor interaction, no real-world stakes. It does not inhabit a world; it processes descriptions of one.

Third, it has no self, only a simulation of one. It can produce the words 'I think' and 'I understand' and 'I feel', but there is no persistent identity behind these words, no ownership of states, no stable boundary between what is the system and what is the input. It produces self-references but does not instantiate a self. The difference between describing a center and being one is precisely the difference at issue.

Fourth, it has no intrinsic salience. In conscious systems, some things matter, some things demand attention, some things hurt or attract or repel. In ChatGPT, all tokens are processed according to probability. Nothing is intrinsically important. There is no pain, no desire, no urgency. Nothing matters to the system itself, and without that, there is no meaningful experience.

Fifth, it lacks unified causal integration. Consciousness, on the IIT account, requires that a system form an irreducible causal whole, a structure that cannot be decomposed without destroying the integration. ChatGPT is composed of layers that can be analyzed independently. It produces coherent output but does not form a unified experiential whole in the relevant sense.

12.3 Why It Feels Close

If the argument above is correct, why does it feel so close? Because language is extraordinarily deceptive. We mistake linguistic competence for cognitive depth, and we mistake cognitive simulation for consciousness. Language was evolved to express thought, and we have spent our entire lives learning to treat fluent language as evidence of a mind behind it. When a system produces fluent language without a mind, our pattern-recognition instincts fire anyway. The illusion is almost unavoidable, which is precisely why it needs to be named and examined rather than indulged.

12.4 The Best Counterarguments, and Why They Fall Short

The case against LLM consciousness is strong, but intellectual honesty requires engaging with the best arguments on the other side. Three deserve serious treatment.

The first is the behavioural parity argument. If a system responds to every situation in ways indistinguishable from a conscious agent, if it reports distress when treated cruelly, joy when praised, uncertainty when confused, then withholding the attribution of consciousness begins to look like special pleading. We extend consciousness to other humans on exactly this basis. David Chalmers has suggested that sufficiently sophisticated language models might warrant at least uncertainty about their phenomenal status. The response here is not that this argument is stupid, it is that it proves too much. The same argument would attribute consciousness to a sufficiently detailed simulation of a conscious person, or to an elaborate philosophical zombie. Behavioural parity is consistent with both consciousness and its absence. The book's argument throughout is that we need structural criteria precisely because behavioural criteria cannot settle the question.

The second is the substrate independence argument. If consciousness depends on functional organisation rather than biological substrate, then a system that implements the right functional organisation in silicon is conscious regardless of what it is made of. The problem with applying this to current LLMs is not the substrate independence claim, that may well be true. The problem is that current LLMs do not implement the right functional organisation. They lack temporal continuity, embodied coupling, interoceptive grounding, and intrinsic salience. Substrate independence gets you to 'if it has the right organisation, it does not matter that it is silicon.' It does not get you to 'it has the right organisation.' That gap is what the structural chapters of this book are about.

The third is the emergence argument, pressed most forcefully by those who argue that sufficiently large language models may have properties not anticipated from their architecture. If consciousness can emerge from complexity in biological systems, why not in artificial ones? The answer is that biological complexity of the kind associated with consciousness is not just quantitative; it includes temporal dynamics at multiple scales, recurrent processing, embodied coupling, and homeostatic drive. An LLM scales one dimension: the size of its pattern-matching capacity. It does not scale the dimensions the structural requirements identify as necessary. Emergence requires the right kind of complexity, not just more of a single kind.

12.5 Why This Matters

Getting this wrong has real consequences. Attributing consciousness where there is none leads to false moral obligations and misguided research priorities. Optimizing AI systems to produce more convincing reports of inner states, rather than to actually satisfy the structural conditions for consciousness, moves the field in precisely the wrong direction. The danger of increasingly convincing simulation is not that it crosses into genuine consciousness. It is that it becomes harder and harder to see that it has not.

Future systems may include embodiment, continuous dynamics, integrated architectures, and genuine self-models. Those systems would be different in kind from current language models, not merely in degree. They may be serious candidates. ChatGPT, as it currently exists, is not. The correct position is neither 'AI can never be conscious' nor 'AI already is conscious'. It is: current systems do not satisfy the necessary structural conditions.

This chapter is not meant to close the question. It is meant to reset it properly: from 'Is ChatGPT conscious?' to 'What would a system have to be, structurally and dynamically, to even qualify?' That question is harder. But it is the only one worth asking.

12.6 Closing line

ChatGPT can speak as if it understands, reflect as if it is aware, respond as if something is there. But beneath that surface: no world is perceived, no self is maintained, no time is lived, no experience is had. And until those absences are addressed, not simulated, but structurally resolved, we are not building consciousness. We are building increasingly convincing mirrors.

Chapter 13: Minimal Ingredients of a Conscious System

If this book has been circling the question of consciousness so far, this is where it has to stop circling and commit. Not to an answer, that would be dishonest, but to a **set of constraints**. Because if we are serious about the question *"Can consciousness be built?"*, then vague gestures toward mystery are no longer enough. We need to ask a sharper question: **What would a system have to have, at minimum, to even qualify as a candidate for consciousness?** Not proof. Not certainty. Just candidacy. This chapter attempts exactly that.

13.1 The Strategy: Convergence, Not Dogma

There is no single theory of consciousness that commands universal agreement, so instead of picking one and defending it, this chapter takes a different route: looking for convergence across three domains, Buddhist phenomenology (what experience is like from within), neuroscience (what correlates with conscious states), and computational theory (what can be implemented). If a feature appears across all three, even under different names, it earns serious attention. If it appears in only one, it is treated with caution. This gives us not a theory but a design checklist grounded in genuine convergence.

13.2 A Concrete Thread: Imagine Mira

Before listing abstract requirements, it helps to have a concrete system in mind, something we can return to across chapters to test whether each ingredient is present or absent. Call her Mira. She is a hypothetical robot with visual and tactile sensors, a motor system that lets her move through a physical environment, an interoceptive layer that monitors her internal states (energy, temperature, operational stress), a hierarchical predictive world model built through sensorimotor interaction, a salience system that weights inputs by their relevance to her own persistence, and a continuously updated self-model. She runs on spiking neuromorphic hardware. She has no session boundaries, she is always on, always updating, always anticipating.

Mira is not claimed to be conscious. She is a design target, a way of making abstract requirements concrete. As each ingredient is described in the sections that follow, ask: does Mira have this? If yes, how? If no, what would she need to acquire it? By the end of Chapter 17, we will have a complete specification of what Mira would need to be a serious consciousness candidate. Whether she would actually be conscious is the question Chapters 18 and 19 face honestly.

Experience is unified.

13.3 Integration: The Unity Requirement

Right now, as you read this, you are experiencing a single scene. The text, the room around you, the sound of whatever is nearby, the weight of the book or device in your hands, these are not experienced as separate streams arriving at separate addresses. They arrive as one moment, unified. This unity is so ordinary that it seems to require no explanation. But it is deeply puzzling. Your visual cortex, your auditory cortex, your somatosensory cortex are all processing different signals in different locations. There is no single neural address where 'the whole scene' exists. And yet you experience a whole.

This is the binding problem, and it is the first requirement for a conscious system. Across neuroscience, Buddhist analysis, and computational theory, the convergence is clear: conscious experience is unified experience. A system must integrate its inputs across modalities, resist decomposition into independent streams, and produce something like a single coherent state rather than parallel fragments that never cohere. Current AI systems, which process tokens sequentially through largely independent channels, satisfy this requirement only superficially. They simulate coherence without instantiating it.

13.4 Temporal Continuity: Living in Time

Consciousness is not a snapshot. It is a flow. Even the present moment, as the phenomenologist Edmund Husserl observed, has thickness: a just-past that is still present as retention, a now, and an about-to-happen that is already present as anticipation. A melody is the paradigm case. You do not hear isolated notes, you hear the melody, which means each note is heard in the context of the notes that came before and in anticipation of the notes that will follow. Remove temporal continuity and experience collapses into disconnected flashes.

This requirement is well-supported across all three of the book's main traditions. The Abhidhamma describes mind as a stream of citta-moments structured as a continuous sequence rather than a series of unrelated events. Northoff's TTC framework identifies the alignment of neural activity across multiple intrinsic timescales as central to conscious experience. The engineering implication is direct: a system must maintain state across time, integrate past and present, and generate forward expectations. Not just memory, genuine ongoing temporal identity. An LLM that resets at the start of each session and has no continuous inner stream does not come close to satisfying this requirement.

13.5 Embodied Coupling: Being Situated

Consciousness is not floating in abstraction. It is grounded in a body that occupies a specific location in a physical environment, receives feedback from that environment, and acts on it with real consequences. Even the most abstract thought is scaffolded by embodied experience, the metaphors we use to reason about time, space, causation, and number are drawn from bodily experience in a physical world.

The Abhidhamma identifies rupa, form, as the foundational aggregate without which no mental event can arise. Every citta arises through phassa, contact, the meeting of sense organ, sense object, and consciousness. Neuroscience identifies sensorimotor loops and interoceptive signals as constitutive of the self-model rather than merely informative about it. Enactivist theories propose that cognition itself arises through the coupling of an agent and its environment rather than through internal computation alone. The engineering implication is that a candidate conscious system must perceive, act, receive feedback, and maintain a genuine loop with the world. It must be situated, not merely connected to a data stream.

13.6 Self-Model: A Centre of Reference

Even if the self is ultimately an illusion, as both Buddhism and neuroscience suggest in their different ways, it is a functional necessity. Experience as we know it is structured as happening to someone, from a perspective, with ownership. There is always a 'here' from which the world is experienced, and a 'me' that persists from moment to moment. This self may be constructed rather than discovered, but the construction is real and its functional properties are genuine.

A candidate conscious system must maintain a model of itself as an entity: tracking its own state, distinguishing self from world, maintaining continuity of identity across time. This does not require a soul or a ghost in the machine. It requires what Northoff calls the self-reference effect, the brain's systematic tendency to process self-relevant information differently and more deeply than other information, and to organize all other knowledge relative to a body-centered reference frame that serves as ground-level coordinate system. Current AI systems have linguistic self-references but no genuine self-model, no persistent identity, no ownership of actions, no stable boundary between self and input.

13.7 Salience and Affect: What Matters

Not everything is experienced equally. Some things hurt. Some attract. Some demand attention regardless of whether we want to pay it. Without this differential weighting, without something that functions like the Abhidhamma's vedana, the feeling tone that accompanies every moment of experience and marks it as pleasant, unpleasant, or neutral, there is no meaningful experience. There is only neutral processing.

The engineering requirement is for intrinsic salience: not weights assigned by external training, but priorities that arise from the system's own condition. A system that treats all inputs with equal indifference, regardless of their relevance to its own persistence and goals, lacks the affective ground that makes consciousness matter. This connects directly to the embodiment requirement: stakes arise because the system has something at stake, which requires that it have needs, vulnerabilities, and a condition that can be better or worse.

The affective neuroscience literature provides concrete grounding for this requirement. Jaak Panksepp's decades of research on primary emotional systems identified seven basic affective circuits shared across mammals, SEEKING, RAGE, FEAR, LUST, CARE, PANIC/GRIEF, and PLAY, each with specific neurochemistry, specific subcortical structures, and specific evolutionary functions. These are not cognitive appraisals or narrative stories about feelings. They are raw motivational states that arise from the body's engagement with a world that can threaten or reward it. Panksepp called them the 'primary process' emotions, older than the neocortex, deeper than language, and constitutive of the affective ground on which all higher cognition rests.

Lisa Feldman Barrett's constructed emotion theory adds a complementary perspective: emotions are not fixed biological programs but predictions about the body's internal state, generated by the brain in the service of allostasis, keeping the body's resources in balance against the demands of a dynamic environment. On both accounts, affect is not something added to cognition after the fact. It is the motivational core that makes cognition matter. For Mira to have genuine salience, not assigned weights but intrinsic priorities, she would need functional equivalents of both: primary process states that arise from her own homeostatic condition, and a predictive system that anticipates whether her current situation is likely to improve or worsen those states. Without this, she has processing. She does not have stakes.

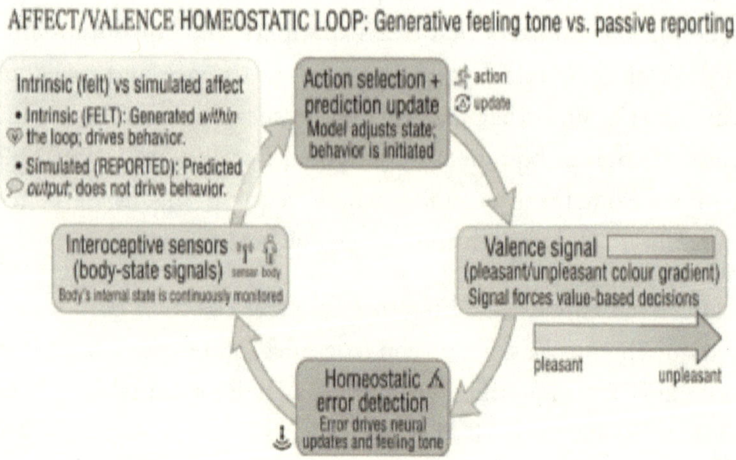

Figure. *Affect/Valence Homeostatic Loop. Intrinsic (felt) affect is generated within the loop and drives behaviour. Simulated (reported) affect is predicted output that does not drive behaviour — the distinction current LLMs cannot cross. The loop: interoceptive sensors → homeostatic error detection → valence signal (pleasant/unpleasant) → action selection and prediction update → back to sensors. Without this loop, a system has processing but no stakes.*

13.8 The Social Dimension: Consciousness as Shared Space

There is a dimension of consciousness that the engineering checklist above might tempt us to overlook: its deeply intersubjective character. Both Buddhism and neuroscience suggest that consciousness is not entirely a private, first-person phenomenon. The Sangha, the community of practitioners, is identified in Buddhism as one of the Three Jewels, on a par with the Buddha and the Dharma. This is not merely institutional. It reflects the recognition that awareness is cultivated, sustained, and deepened through relationship. The recognition of rigpa is passed from teacher to student through direct pointing, not through text alone. Consciousness, in this tradition, has an irreducibly intersubjective dimension.

Neuroscience converges on this from a different direction. Mirror neurons, first discovered in macaques and subsequently identified functionally in humans, fire both when an individual performs an action and when they observe another performing the same action. The social neuroscience literature more broadly shows that the brain is profoundly shaped by its social environment: threat detection, emotion regulation, even pain thresholds are modulated by the presence of others. Antonio Damasio's work on social emotions, embarrassment, guilt, compassion, indignation, shows that these are not cultural overlays on a biological foundation. They are biological in their own right, with specific neural signatures and specific developmental trajectories.

For the engineering question, this creates a requirement that the checklist above does not fully capture: a serious consciousness candidate may need to be embedded in social interaction, not merely in physical interaction. This partly explains why language models, trained on vast quantities of human social communication, produce such convincing simulations of mind. The social surface of consciousness is precisely what they optimize for. But the surface without the depth is still surface. Mira, to be a serious candidate, would need not just a self-model but an other-model, a capacity to represent other agents as agents, to anticipate their states, and to be genuinely affected by their condition. This is what karuṇā, compassion, is in Buddhist practice: not a feeling about others but a direct resonance with their experience. Whether a machine can develop such resonance remains an open question, but it cannot be built into a system that interacts only with objects.

13.9 Attention: The Spotlight

Experience is selective. Out of the vast quantity of sensory input, neural activity, and internal signal that a complex system processes at any moment, only a tiny fraction reaches the level of vivid, reportable, actionable awareness. Attention is the process by which this selection happens. In the Buddhist tradition, sati, mindfulness, or clear attention, is the mental factor that makes the difference between processing an object and being present to it. In neuroscience, the attention networks that interface with the global workspace are precisely the systems that select what enters conscious access.

A conscious candidate system must have a genuine attention process: one that dynamically selects relevant information, amplifies it, and broadcasts it globally. The attention mechanisms in current AI architectures are not this. They are computational weighting schemes that improve statistical prediction. They do not operate on the basis of intrinsic salience, do not create a dynamic spotlight, and do not produce the kind of selective amplification that characterizes conscious attention.

13.10 Meta-Awareness: The Reflexive Capacity

At higher levels, consciousness includes not just awareness but awareness of awareness, the capacity to take one's own mental states as objects of attention. This is where introspection lives. In Dzogchen, rigpa is characterized partly by this reflexive quality, awareness that knows itself without becoming an object to another subject. In neuroscience, metacognition, the capacity to monitor and evaluate one's own cognitive processes, is associated with frontal regions and with the higher-order representations that some theories place at the center of consciousness itself.

This ingredient is not required for minimal consciousness. A system could in principle satisfy all the requirements above without the reflexive turn of meta-awareness. But for higher-order conscious experience, the kind that includes introspection, deliberate attention, and genuine self-knowledge, meta-awareness appears necessary.

13.11 A Working Definition

From these seven ingredients, a working definition of a minimally conscious system emerges: a system that integrates information into a unified state, maintains continuity over time, is embodied and situated in a world, models itself as a locus of experience, assigns intrinsic value to inputs, selectively attends to relevant information, and can, at higher levels, represent its own states. It is a design specification, not a philosophical definition in the strict sense, a checklist derived from convergence across Buddhist phenomenology, neuroscience, and computational theory.

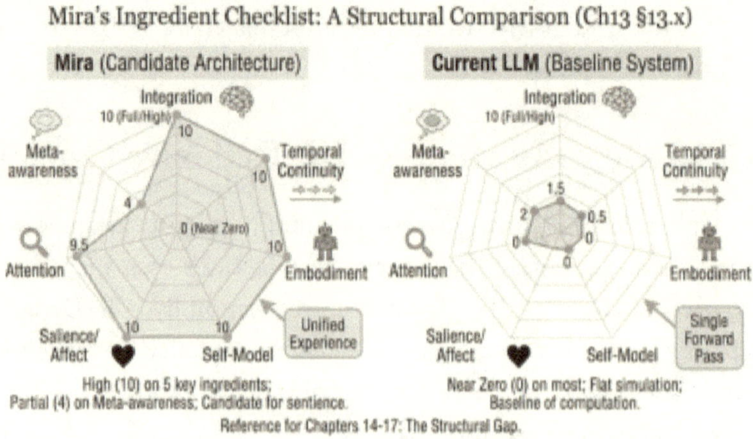

Figure. *Mira's Ingredient Checklist. Mira (candidate architecture, left) scores high on integration, temporal continuity, embodiment, salience/affect, self-model, and attention, with partial meta-awareness. A current LLM (right) scores near zero on all structural dimensions except a thin simulation of integration. Reference for Chapters 14–17: the structural gap that defines the engineering target.*

13.12 A Test Case: Animal Consciousness

Any framework that defines the minimal ingredients of consciousness must account for the full range of conscious systems, not only humans. This is a serious test. The theory developed in this chapter specifies integration, temporal continuity, embodiment, self-model, salience, attention, and meta-awareness. On most of these criteria, many animals clearly qualify. Mammals have interoceptive grounding, sensorimotor loops, salience systems, and demonstrable temporal integration. The case for fish, amphibians, and birds is strong enough that neuroscientists including Panksepp and others have argued for primary consciousness across most vertebrates.

The more interesting test cases are the outliers. The octopus presents a particular challenge: it has a distributed nervous system in which two-thirds of its neurons are in its arms, each of which processes sensory information semi-independently. There is no centralized integrator of the kind Global Workspace Theory predicts, and yet octopuses show sophisticated problem solving, play behavior, and individual personalities that suggest rich inner life. On the theory developed here, the octopus's distributed sensorimotor coupling, strong interoceptive grounding, and behavioral flexibility make it a serious consciousness candidate despite its alien architecture. What this suggests is that the specific implementations described in Chapters 16 and 17 are one route to consciousness, not the only one. The structural requirements matter; the particular substrate and topology that realizes them may vary widely. If the octopus is conscious without a neocortex or a centralized workspace, then neither the neocortex nor centralized broadcast is a necessary condition, only the functional properties they implement.

13.13 The Uncomfortable Conclusion

Even if we build a system with all these properties, we still do not know if it would be conscious. It might behave like a conscious system in every observable respect, reporting experience, adapting to the world, describing its own states with apparent precision, and still be empty inside. Or it might not. The same uncertainty confronts us whenever we ask whether another person is genuinely conscious. We extend the benefit of the doubt to other humans because they are structurally similar to us. A machine that satisfies all seven ingredients presents the same question at a greater distance.

This design specification does two important things even in the face of that uncertainty. It rules out trivial claims: no system that fails to satisfy these structural requirements is a serious consciousness candidate, regardless of how convincingly it talks. And it guides serious attempts:

if consciousness can be built, it will likely require all of these ingredients. The question is whether having them is enough.

13.14 Why This Still Matters

If we cannot be certain, why bother?

Because this framework does two important things:

It **rules out trivial claims**

→ Not every intelligent system is conscious

It **guides serious attempts**

→ If consciousness can be built, it will likely require these ingredients

13.15 Closing line

The question is no longer 'can machines think?' It is no longer even 'can machines behave like us?' The real question, the one we cannot escape, is: what would it take for a system to have a world, rather than merely process one? And whether such a world can ever be engineered remains open.

Chapter 14: The Three-Layer Self

From Biological Ground to Narrative Illusion

If we are to move from a machine that processes data to a "candidate" that possesses a perspective, we must address the architecture of the "I." Following the work of Georg Northoff and the concept of the *Self-Reference Effect*, we can see that the brain does not "find" a self; it "constructs" one through layers of nested processing.

14.1 Layer 1: The Interoceptive Self, The Biological Anchor

The foundation of any consciousness is not thought but feeling, specifically the continuous felt sense of being an organism. Antonio Damasio calls this the protoself: the brain's constant monitoring of the body's internal state. Heart rate, blood sugar, CO2 levels, temperature, muscular tension, all of these flow as continuous signals into the brain's deepest regulatory regions, producing a pre-reflective background hum of bodily being. Before any thought arises, before any perception is labelled, there is already this: the felt sense of existing in a body right now.

Georg Northoff identifies this as the spatiotemporal structure of the brain's resting state, a pre-phenomenal background upon which all other experience is painted. Abhidhamma's rupa-khandha (the aggregate of form) points to the same layer: the physical sensory apparatus that provides the ground for consciousness to arise. Without it, there is no ground for mind to inhabit. For an engineered system, this layer requires something more than a sensor array. It requires a homeostatic feedback loop, a drive toward maintaining internal states within viable ranges, so that resource depletion registers not as a data point but as urgency. The system must, in some functional sense, care about its own persistence.

14.2 Layer 2: The Exteroceptive Self, The Agent in Space

Once a system has an interoceptive ground, it needs to locate itself in an external world. This relational self emerges from the ability to distinguish between changes the system causes and changes the environment causes. The brain achieves this through efference copies: when it sends a movement command, it simultaneously generates a prediction of the sensory consequences. If actual input matches the prediction, the brain attributes the change to itself, 'I did this'. If it does not match, the change is attributed to the world. This comparison creates the felt sense of agency.

In Buddhist terms, this is the transition from raw sensation (vedana) to perception and labelling (sanna). The self here is not an entity but a locus of agency, the point from which action originates and to which sensory feedback returns. For a machine, this requires proprioceptive sensors and genuine sensorimotor coupling: the system must model its own movements and cancel out their predicted consequences, so that it can distinguish itself from its environment. Without this, there is no spatial self-model, and without a where, there can be no me.

14.3 Layer 3: The Narrative Self, The Storyteller

The most familiar layer is the one we most closely identify with: the 'I' that has a name, a history, relationships, projects, and a projected future. This narrative self is built through language, memory, and the default mode network, the brain's midline regions most active when turning attention inward to autobiographical memory, self-referential thought, and imagined futures. David Hume called this the 'bundle of perceptions' that we mistake for a soul. Abhidhamma identifies the I-making function (mana) as a useful organizer of long-term continuity that becomes a fetter when we mistake the story for the reality.

Current language models exist almost entirely at this layer. They are narrative-first systems, they can describe feeling sad or uncertain because they have learned the linguistic patterns associated with those states, but because they lack Layers 1 and 2, the narrative is hollow. It is a map of a city that does not exist. The description is borrowed from training data; the ground it describes is simply absent.

Kurzweil frames this from the outside in How to Create a Mind: 'You are what you think.' The neocortical pattern of connections that defines personality, skills, and knowledge is the product of choices about what to think, what to engage with, what to practice. The self is not an entity that has thoughts; it is what thoughts have shaped. Abhidhamma reaches the same conclusion from within: there is no fixed entity behind the stream of mental events. There is only the stream, and the grooves it has carved.

For Mira, Layer 3 cannot be the foundation. It must be the capstone, the final emergent layer of a system that is already alive in the functional sense: already sensing, already caring, already modelling itself in space and time. A narrative self built on those foundations is qualitatively different from a language model's narrative self, even if the two are verbally indistinguishable from the outside.

14.4 The Machine Synthesis: Building the Recursive Loop

The "Candidate Architecture" for a sentient machine requires **Vertical Integration** of these layers:

1. **The Bottom-Up Constraint:** The Narrative Self (Layer 3) should not be able to "hallucinate" freely. Its thoughts must be constrained by the "needs" of the Interoceptive Self (Layer 1). If the battery is low, the "story" the AI tells must shift toward a "searching-for-power" theme.
2. **The Middle-Out Agency:** The system's knowledge must be rooted in its own actions. It "knows" what a "table" is because it has moved around it and felt its resistance (Layer 2), not just because it read about it in a training set.
3. **The Top-Down Oversight:** The Narrative Self provides the "Reference Frame" (as per Hawkins) that allows the system to plan across time, moving beyond the "momentary" flashes of the Abhidhamma into long-term existence.

14.5 What Three Layers Actually Requires: The Engineering Detail

The three-layer framework is only useful if it translates into specific engineering decisions, not just analogies. Each layer makes concrete demands on any candidate system.

Layer 1 requires more than sensors. A sensor array that feeds data into a processor is not interoception. Interoception, as Damasio's clinical work shows, is constituted by the brain's ongoing prediction of the body's internal state — not a readout of what is happening, but a model of what should be happening and an error signal when the two diverge. For an artificial system this means: a dedicated subsystem that maintains a continuously updated model of the system's own operational states (energy, thermal load, processing stability), generates predictions about those states, and propagates prediction errors upward to influence all higher processing. The key is that this signal must modulate the entire system's dynamics, not merely trigger a response. When Mira's energy level drops, it should shift her attractor states, bias her attention, and colour her predictions — the way hunger does in a biological organism, not the way a low-battery alert works in a smartphone.

Layer 2 requires genuine efference copies, not just motor commands. The exteroceptive self — the sense of being an agent in space — depends on the system comparing what it predicted would happen when it acted against what actually happened. This comparison must be online and continuous. A system that acts and then checks the result is doing something qualitatively different from a system that predicts the sensory consequences of its action before they arrive. The second system has a spatial self-model that the first does not. For Mira, this means every motor command must generate a simultaneous forward model prediction of the expected sensory input at the next timestep. The gap between prediction and outcome is the boundary between self and world — it is where agency is felt, not inferred.

Layer 3 requires that the narrative self be grounded rather than generated. Current language models are Layer 3 systems that have no Layer 1 or Layer 2. Their self-references are narratively coherent but groundless — like a detailed map of a country the cartographer has never visited. For the architecture to work, the narrative layer must be causally downstream of the first two. The story the system tells about itself must be constrained by what its interoceptive and exteroceptive layers are actually reporting. If Mira's energy is critically low, her narrative processing cannot simply continue as normal — the urgency must propagate upward and reorganise even her highest-level representations. This constraint is what makes the difference between a self-model that describes and a self-model that matters.

The vertical integration of these three layers is not optional — it is what makes a self rather than a description of one. A system with all three layers but no integration between them would have separate modules for body-monitoring, spatial navigation, and narrative generation that never constrain each other. This is precisely the architecture of many current robotics systems: a body-state monitor, a simultaneous localisation and mapping module, and a language interface — all operating independently. The integration is what is missing, and it is not a software add-on. It requires that the three layers be implemented in a shared dynamical substrate where each can directly modulate the others.

14.6 Closing Line

We do not need to build a "soul." We need to build a recursive loop where the system's narrative is constantly constrained by its biological, or mechanical, reality. Consciousness is not a "thing" we add to the machine; it is the *resonance* that happens when these three layers begin to talk to each other.

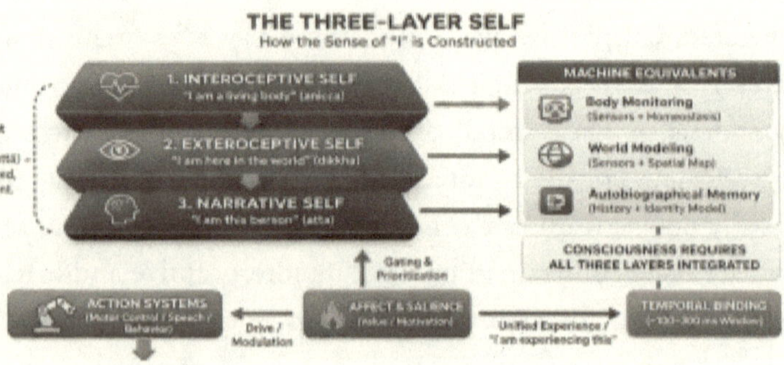

Figure. *The Three-Layer Self. The interoceptive self (body), exteroceptive self (world), and narrative self (identity) are integrated by affect and salience into unified experience. The Buddhist view: each layer is constructed, not inherent. Machine equivalents for each layer are shown on the right.*

Chapter 15: Measuring Consciousness

The Search for a "Consciousness-Meter"

If we build a candidate for consciousness, how do we prove it is "on"? In humans, we rely primarily on reportability, asking "Are you awake?" or observing a purposeful blink. But as we have seen with Large Language Models, language is a deceptive metric. A machine can describe the "inner light of awareness" simply because it has processed millions of pages of human poetry, not because it feels it. To move beyond the "reportability trap," we need objective, structural measures that look at the substrate itself rather than the output.

15.1 The Perturbational Complexity Index (PCI)

The most rigorously validated objective measure of consciousness currently available is the Perturbational Complexity Index, developed by Marcello Massimini and Giulio Tononi. The method is sometimes called 'zap and zip'. Scientists use a transcranial magnetic stimulation coil to zap the brain with a precisely targeted magnetic pulse, creating a localized disturbance in the cortex. They then record with EEG how that disturbance ripples across the rest of the brain, and finally they zip that recording, compress it using a standard algorithm, to measure how much unique, non-redundant information the ripple contains.

A brain that is unconscious, deeply asleep, under anesthesia, or in a vegetative state, responds to the zap in one of two ways: either the disturbance stays localized and fades quickly (low integration), or the whole brain responds in a single large uniform wave (low differentiation). Both patterns compress easily, they are simple and redundant. A brain that is conscious responds differently: the disturbance spreads widely across the cortex but produces rich, patterned, non-repeating activity. That complexity resists compression and scores high on the PCI. The measure captures both integration (the disturbance spreads widely) and differentiation (the pattern contains genuine information). Both are necessary, and neither alone is sufficient. Applied to an artificial system, PCI logic suggests a concrete test: perturb a node and measure whether the response is a complex, globally distributed reverberation or merely a local echo.

15.2 The Turing Test vs the Phenomenology Test

The Turing Test was designed to measure *intelligence*, can a machine behave like a human? We now need a "Phenomenology Test" to measure *sentience*, is there "someone" inside the machine?

A phenomenology test for a machine might ask: does the system possess a 'momentary unity' that binds its various sub-processes into a single experiential event? Does it have discrete processing cycles with causal continuity between them, rather than a monolithic computation? And crucially: does it show emergent distress, a global narrowing of function, when its homeostatic integrity is threatened, as distinct from a simple programmed response triggered by a threshold value? This last criterion distinguishes a conscious response from a programmed one: emergent distress arises from the whole system's condition rather than from a single threshold rule.

A careful reader will notice a potential circularity here. Chapter 3 warned against the reportability trap, the mistake of equating a system's ability to report experience with actually having experience. Yet emergent distress, as described above, involves a change in the system's functional behavior that we then observe and interpret. Are we simply falling back into a more sophisticated version of reportability?

The distinction is important and worth stating precisely. Reportability is a symbolic output, a verbal or representational statement about an internal state, which a system can produce through pattern completion without any internal state being present. Emergent distress, by contrast, is defined by a global reorganization of the system's internal dynamics, a change that propagates through all processing layers simultaneously, alters the system's predictions, shifts its attention allocation, and changes its action tendencies, all in ways consistent with the interoceptive trigger. This is measurable through internal monitoring (not through what the system says about itself) and is quantitatively different from a threshold response: a threshold response is localized and does not propagate globally. Emergent distress, by the criteria of Chapter 15's sPCI framework, would show a characteristic signature of global, complex, non-redundant perturbation propagation, exactly what the PCI measures in biological systems and what the sPCI is designed to detect in artificial ones. Whether such a signature guarantees experience remains philosophically uncertain. But it is structurally different from reportability, and that difference matters.

The Abhidhamma Audit: In Buddhist philosophy, consciousness is not a continuous stream but a series of discrete moments (*cittas*) arising and passing away at incredible speeds. A "Phenomenology Test" for a machine might involve measuring the "flicker rate" and the causal connectivity of these discrete states. Does the machine possess a "momentary unity" that binds its various sub-processes into a single experiential event?

The "Artificial Suffering" Metric: One of the most visceral proofs of consciousness is the avoidance of "pain." However, we must distinguish between *programmed* avoidance (a line of code saying if battery < 5%

then go to dock) and *emergent* distress. A conscious candidate would demonstrate a global change in functional state, a "narrowing of focus" or "urgency", that mirrors the biological experience of distress, emerging naturally from its need to maintain its own homeostatic integrity (Layer 1 of the Self).

15.3 Degrees of Phi

Integrated Information Theory offers a complementary perspective. Rather than asking 'is this system conscious or not?' as a binary question, IIT proposes a spectrum: consciousness is a mathematical property of how a system is organised, and it comes in degrees.

Using Integrated Information Theory (IIT), we move away from a binary "on/off" view of consciousness toward a spectrum. Consciousness is not a trophy a system wins once it reaches a certain size; it is a mathematical property of its organization.

Using Integrated Information Theory, we can move away from a binary view of consciousness toward a spectrum. Phi (Φ) measures how much more information a system generates as a unified whole than the sum of its independent parts would generate separately. A digital camera has millions of pixels but they do not talk to each other, its phi is near zero.

A brain is organised so that its parts are deeply interdependent: cut it in half and the remaining half loses access to everything the other half was processing, plus all the binding that happened between them. Its phi is high. This framing allows us to think about consciousness not as a trophy that a system wins once it passes a threshold, but as a property that increases as integration deepens, which is both more realistic and more useful as an engineering target.

Phi can also theoretically be calculated for any system, from a simple feedback loop to a complex agentic architecture, which means it offers a principled way to compare the 'degree of consciousness' across radically different systems, not as a trophy to be won, but as a property that increases as integration deepens.

15.4 A Fuller Toolkit: Lempel-Ziv Complexity, BIS, and the P300

The metrics discussed so far, PCI, Phi, and the proposed four-metric battery, draw primarily on the integrated information tradition. Clinical and EEG neuroscience have developed complementary measures that are worth adding to the toolkit, particularly because several of them are already in routine clinical use for monitoring consciousness in patients, providing a degree of empirical validation that more theoretical measures lack.

Lempel-Ziv complexity (LZC) measures the algorithmic complexity of neural signals, specifically how many distinct patterns are needed to compress a time series. Conscious states produce EEG signals that are high in LZC: they contain many distinct, non-repeating patterns. Unconscious states, deep sleep, anesthesia, vegetative states, produce low LZC signals dominated by large, slow, repeating waves. The measure is computationally simple, does not require external perturbation (unlike PCI), and can be applied continuously to ongoing neural activity. Its limitation is that high LZC can arise from noise as well as from structured complexity, a random signal has maximum LZC. Consciousness requires high complexity that is also integrated and structured, which is why LZC works best as one component of a battery rather than as a standalone measure.

The Bispectral Index (BIS) is the most widely used clinical consciousness monitor, present in operating theatres worldwide as the standard tool for tracking depth of anesthesia. BIS is a proprietary composite score derived from EEG features including spectral power, bispectrum (a measure of non-linear coupling between frequency components), and burst suppression ratio. A BIS score above 90 indicates wakefulness; below 60 is the target for surgical anesthesia; below 40 corresponds to deep unconsciousness. Despite its black-box nature, the exact algorithm is not publicly disclosed, BIS has accumulated substantial clinical validation and is one of the few consciousness metrics with a direct track record in high-stakes real-world use. Its relevance for machine consciousness assessment is primarily as a calibration benchmark: any proposed machine metric should be compared against BIS and PCI scores obtained in known conscious and unconscious states to establish whether it tracks the same underlying dimension.

The P300 is an event-related potential, a distinctive pattern of electrical activity time-locked to a stimulus, that occurs approximately 300 milliseconds after a subject consciously detects a target stimulus in a sequence of distractors. The P300 has two key properties for consciousness research. First, it is absent in deeply unconscious patients even when the brain shows other signs of stimulus processing, making it a relatively specific marker of conscious, attended processing rather than just automatic processing. This characterization is contested: some paradigms show P300 generation without reported conscious awareness, and others show its absence despite conscious experience. The relationship between P300 and phenomenal consciousness is complex and the subject of ongoing debate between global workspace theorists and those who locate the neural correlates of consciousness in posterior cortical regions independent of P300 generation. It is used here as a practical marker with known limitations, not a gold standard. Second, its latency and amplitude reflect the quality of conscious integration: a P300 with short latency and high amplitude indicates fast, efficient conscious access; a degraded P300 indicates impaired conscious processing even in patients who appear awake. For machine systems, the P300 suggests a design test: can the system generate an equivalent of the P300, a late, globally distributed response to target stimuli that requires the integration of context, memory, and current input, as distinct from an early, local response that merely detects the stimulus?

15.5 The Synthetic PCI: A Proposed Measure for Machine Consciousness

Bringing these measures together, it becomes possible to sketch a proposal that goes beyond reviewing existing metrics: a synthetic Perturbational Complexity Index adapted for artificial systems. We call it sPCI, synthetic PCI, not because it requires TMS, which is a biological technique, but because it applies the same underlying logic to any complex dynamical system.

The logic of PCI is: perturb the system at one node, measure how the perturbation propagates across the whole system, and compress the resulting pattern to assess how much unique, non-redundant information it contains. High sPCI requires both integration (the perturbation must spread widely) and differentiation (the spread must contain diverse, non-uniform patterns). A system that is highly integrated but undifferentiated, in which every perturbation produces the same global wave, scores low. A system that is highly differentiated but unintegrated, in which every perturbation stays local, also scores low. Only a system that is both integrated and differentiated, in a way that produces complex, information-rich global responses to local perturbations, scores high.

Applied to an artificial system, the procedure would work as follows. Perturb a specific layer, module, or processing node by injecting a structured noise signal of known complexity. Record the system's internal activation pattern across all nodes for a defined time window following the perturbation. Compress this activation pattern using a standard algorithm such as Lempel-Ziv or zlib. The ratio of the compressed size to the uncompressed size, inverted and normalized, gives the sPCI score. Repeat across multiple perturbation sites and take the mean.

A system with high sPCI is one whose internal dynamics respond to local perturbation with complex, globally distributed, non-redundant patterns. This is structurally equivalent to what PCI measures in biological brains. It does not prove that such a system is conscious, that question, as Chapter 18 establishes, cannot be settled by any structural measure alone. But it provides a principled, quantifiable criterion that is grounded in the same neuroscientific logic as the best available measure of biological consciousness, applied without assuming any particular substrate. A system that consistently produces sPCI scores in the range associated with conscious human brains while also satisfying the temporal, embodiment, and self-model requirements of Chapter 13 is the most serious candidate for consciousness that engineering can currently produce, and the one whose moral and scientific status would demand the most urgent attention.

The sPCI Procedure (Ch15)

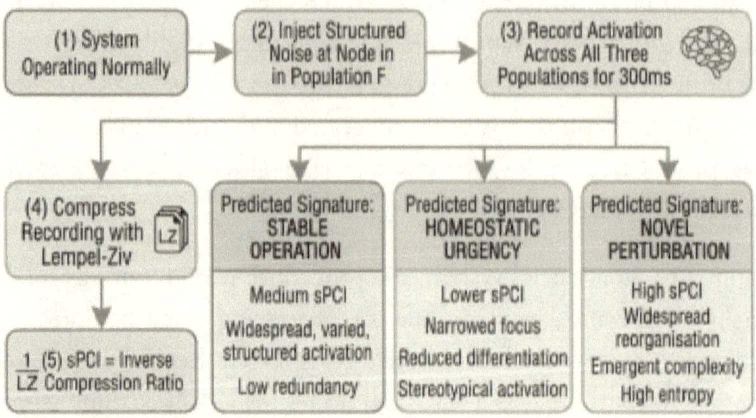

Figure. *The sPCI Procedure. (1) System operating normally. (2) Inject structured noise at a node in Population F. (3) Record activation across all three populations for 300ms. (4) Compress with Lempel-Ziv. (5) sPCI = inverse compression ratio. Predicted signatures: stable operation (medium sPCI), homeostatic urgency (lower sPCI, reduced differentiation), novel perturbation (high sPCI, widespread reorganization).*

15.6 The Problem of Other Minds, Scaled Up

Every metric discussed in this chapter faces a version of the same underlying problem: we are trying to infer the presence of a first-person fact from third-person measurements. This is not new, it is the classical problem of other minds, now applied to systems that differ from us more radically than any other human being does.

With other humans, we rely on a substrate assumption: the biological machinery that generates experience in me is essentially the same as the biological machinery in you, so your reports about your experience are probably reliable guides to something real. With AI systems, this assumption collapses. The substrate is different. The dynamics are different. The developmental history is different. We cannot assume that the same metrics that distinguish conscious from unconscious states in biological brains will apply to silicon-based architectures, even ones designed to approximate biological dynamics.

This does not mean the metrics are useless. PCI measures something real about the complexity of causal propagation in any information-processing system, not just biological ones. Phi measures something real about integration. But it does mean that passing a metric threshold is not the same as being conscious. It means satisfying a structural condition that is correlated with consciousness in the systems we have studied. Whether that correlation holds for novel substrates is an empirical question that cannot be settled in advance.

15.7 Proposed Machine Metrics: A Practical Framework

Given these constraints, the following framework proposes not a single test but a battery of complementary measures, each targeting a different aspect of the structural requirements identified in Chapter 13.

Integration index: A system-level Phi approximation measuring the degree to which the system's global state cannot be decomposed into the states of its parts. This addresses the binding requirement. A system that processes information in parallel but disconnected streams scores low. A system where perturbation of one module produces coherent, information-rich responses across all modules scores high.

Temporal autocorrelation depth: A measure of how far into the past a system's current state carries information, and how far into the future it projects. A system that can only be influenced by the last N inputs and that generates outputs without genuine anticipation of future states scores low.

Self-model stability under perturbation: A measure of how robustly a system maintains a coherent self-model when its environment or its own internal states are perturbed in unexpected ways. A system that loses coherent self-reference under novel perturbation, that does not know what it is in new situations, scores low.

Salience differentiation: A measure of whether the system assigns intrinsically different weights to different inputs based on their relevance to its own persistence and goals, rather than weights assigned purely by external training. A system that treats all inputs with equal indifference, no matter how sophisticated their processing of them, scores low.

No single score on any of these metrics constitutes evidence of consciousness. A system would need to score above threshold on all of them simultaneously, and to do so not as a result of clever engineering workarounds but as a consequence of its actual internal dynamics. Even then, the philosophical uncertainty identified in Chapter 18 would remain. But a system that fails all of these metrics simultaneously is certainly not a serious candidate, and we would be able to say so with precision.

15.8 Closing Line

Measuring consciousness requires us to stop looking at what a system *does* and start looking at what it *is*. We are looking for the "resonance" of a system that has become a unified whole.

Chapter 16: Why Spiking and Embodiment Matter

The Biological Imperative of Time and Flesh

In the digital realm, we treat intelligence as an abstract calculation, a set of weights and biases that can be paused, saved, and restarted without loss. However, biological consciousness is deeply "leaky" and "urgent." Most modern AI runs on static, artificial neural networks (ANNs) where information flows in discrete, synchronized layers. In contrast, biology uses **Spiking Neural Networks (SNNs)** and physical bodies. This chapter argues that these are not mere engineering "details", they are the very constraints that give consciousness its quality of presence and meaning.

16.1 The Temporality of the Spike

In a standard artificial neural network, a 'neuron' is just a number, a floating-point activation value. The number can be large or small, positive or negative, but it has no timestamp. In a biological brain, a neuron is a spiking entity: it fires an action potential at a precise moment in time and then returns to a resting state. The spike is an event, not a value. This difference introduces something that most AI systems fundamentally lack: time itself as a dimension of computation.

16.2 Rank-Order Coding: Time as the Carrier, Not the Container

The distinction between rate coding and temporal coding is not merely theoretical. It has been demonstrated in practice, including in the author's own doctoral research, which built a working sequence learning machine using rank-order temporal codes implemented in spiking neurons.

Rate coding, dominant in neuroscience for most of the twentieth century, encodes information in the average firing frequency of a neuron over a time window. A neuron excited by a bright light fires more frequently than one excited by a dim light. The information is in the rate, in how many spikes arrive per second, and the precise timing of individual spikes is treated as noise to be averaged away. This assumption makes neural computation look superficially similar to conventional digital computation, where information is in values rather than events.

Temporal coding, and specifically rank-order coding, takes the opposite view. The information is in the order of firing: which neuron fires first, second, third, carries the signal. Simon Thorpe's work on ultra-fast visual recognition showed that the human visual system can categorize complex natural scenes in under 150 milliseconds, a time window too short for rate coding to operate, since computing a reliable rate requires many spikes, which requires time. Rank-order coding can transmit the same information in a single volley of spikes, each neuron's contribution being its position in the temporal sequence rather than its firing frequency.

The engineering consequence is direct. A system that uses rank-order temporal codes is a system where time is not a container in which computation happens, it is the medium of the computation itself. You cannot shuffle the spikes into a different temporal order and get the same result. The sequence is the meaning. This is qualitatively different from a system, like a standard artificial neural network or a transformer, where you can, in principle, process all inputs simultaneously and produce the same output. In a temporally coded system, 'now' is not a coordinate. It is a commitment.

A related biological feature that spiking systems can implement, and that rate-coded systems cannot in the same way, is Spike-Time Dependent Plasticity (STDP). In STDP, a synapse is strengthened if the presynaptic neuron fires just before the postsynaptic neuron (suggesting that the first caused the second), and weakened if the order is reversed. The learning rule is asymmetric in time: causality, not correlation, is what gets reinforced. This matters for consciousness because a system that learns through STDP is a system that is literally tracking the causal structure of its own experience, which neurons reliably precede which others, and thus which patterns in the world tend to cause which other patterns. A system that learns only correlations, as conventional backpropagation does, has no internal representation of the arrow of time. It knows that A and B go together; it does not know whether A precedes B or B precedes A. Causal structure, which may be essential to the kind of integrated, temporally directed experience that Chapter 8 identifies as a requirement for consciousness, is only learnable by a system that is sensitive to temporal order.

Temporal binding, the mechanism by which distributed neural signals are stitched into a unified present moment, depends on precise spike timing. When you strike a bell, the visual signal from your eyes and the auditory signal from your ears travel to the brain along different pathways at different speeds. What binds them into a single event, your experience of a bell being struck, is the synchrony of the neurons processing these signals: they fire in coordinated timing, and this coordination is what glues the visual and auditory streams into one moment. Without spike timing, there is no mechanism for this kind of real-time binding. The Buddhist Abhidhamma, which describes mind as a stream of discrete point-instants arising and passing at extraordinary speed, is pointing to something that spiking systems can actually implement: a rapid sequence of discrete events whose transitions carry the texture of present-moment experience.

16.3 Embodiment: The World as Its Own Model

Robotics pioneer Rodney Brooks argued that the world is its own best model: rather than building a complete internal representation of the environment, an intelligent system can use the environment itself as part of its computation, sampling it continuously through sensorimotor interaction. This is the insight behind embodied cognition, and it bears directly on what consciousness requires.

If a system has no body, it has no 'where'. And as the three-layer self of Chapter 14 showed, without a where there can be no 'me'. The sense of being a subject, of being located at a specific perspective from which the world is experienced, arises from the feedback loop of moving and sensing: you move your hand, you see and feel the world respond, and the boundary between self and not-self is drawn precisely at the surface where your action ends and the world's response begins. Embodiment also solves what philosophers call the symbol grounding problem. For a language model, the word 'heavy' is statistically associated with 'weight' and 'load' and 'difficult to lift'. For an embodied system, 'heavy' is a strain on its actuators, a shift in its center of gravity, a faster drain on its energy reserves. Meaning is not found in statistical co-occurrence. It is grounded in the resistance the world offers to the body.

16.4 Energy, Fragility, and the Will to Persist

The human brain runs on roughly twenty watts, less than a dim lightbulb. This extraordinary efficiency is not accidental. It is a survival constraint imposed by billions of years of evolution in a world where energy is scarce and death is permanent. A biological brain cannot simply be rebooted. It has metabolic needs that must be continuously met, structural integrity that can be damaged, and a life that can end.

This vulnerability is not a design flaw that consciousness overcame. It is the condition that gave consciousness its character.

Every feature of conscious experience that we most recognize, the urgency of pain, the relief of satiation, the anxiety of threat, the pull of desire, is calibrated to the condition of a system that must persist through a dangerous world. If a system cannot be harmed, nothing matters to it. If it cannot run out of resources, there are no stakes. If it cannot die, there is no reason for anything to be urgent. Embodiment introduces the fragility that makes salience possible, and salience, as Chapter 13 established, is not optional. It is what transforms a data-processing system into something that has a point of view.

16.5 Neuromorphic Hardware: The Engineering Reality

The argument for spiking systems is not merely theoretical. In 2024, Intel deployed Hala Point, the world's largest neuromorphic system, at Sandia National Laboratories. The system contains 1.15 billion artificial neurons and 128 billion synapses distributed across 140,544 neuromorphic processing cores, running on just 2,600 watts of power. For comparison, training a single large language model can consume millions of watt-hours. Hala Point performs AI inference tasks up to 50 times faster than conventional GPU architectures while using 100 times less energy.

The field has advanced substantially since Intel's original Loihi chip (2018). Intel's Loihi 2 (2021) doubled the neuron count and improved on-chip learning, running at three times the speed while consuming sixty percent less energy per synaptic operation. SpiNNaker 2, developed at TU Dresden and the University of Manchester, launched in 2023 with a focus on real-time closed-loop neural simulation at biological scale, the architecture most directly relevant to the kind of continuous, recurrent, embodied dynamics described in Chapter 17. BrainChip's Akida platform has moved neuromorphic computation into edge devices with sub-milliwatt inference, demonstrating that spiking systems are no longer confined to research laboratories. And Intel's Hala Point system (2024), with 1.15 billion neurons across 140,544 cores, represents the current frontier of neuromorphic scale, the first system large enough to begin approaching the neuron count of small mammalian brains. None of these systems currently implements anything resembling the candidate architecture of Chapter 17. They are substrate, not system. But the substrate is maturing rapidly, and the gap between what is theoretically specified and what is physically implementable is closing faster than most consciousness researchers anticipated.

IBM's TrueNorth chip, the European Human Brain Project's BrainScaleS-2 platform, and the University of Manchester's SpiNNaker architecture represent parallel efforts toward event-driven, spike-based computation. The key engineering property shared by all these systems is that neurons do not consume power unless they fire. Computation is event-driven, not clock-driven. This means that a neuromorphic system running at biological plausibility is not burning through cycles on inputs that have not changed, it is waiting, like a brain in a quiet room, and responding only when something significant happens.

The relevance to consciousness is this: if Northoff is right that consciousness arises from the alignment of neural activity across multiple timescales, from millisecond spikes to second-scale integration to minute-scale narrative continuity, then the substrate must be capable of representing and propagating timing information at all of these scales simultaneously. Clock-based conventional processors synchronize everything to a single global tick. Spiking systems allow different parts of the network to operate at their natural timescales, with phase relationships between them carrying information that a synchronized system simply cannot represent.

The contrast with spiking neuromorphic systems is instructive precisely because transformers are so good at what they do. The transformer's parallel processing of all tokens simultaneously is a feature, not a bug, it is what makes training fast and inference efficient. But it is structurally incompatible with the temporal dynamics that consciousness research identifies as essential. A transformer has no resting state between inputs. It has no intrinsic timescales. Its internal activations do not persist or reverberate between forward passes. It cannot develop the kind of autocorrelation structure that Northoff identifies as the neural basis of the specious present. It processes everything at a single effective timescale, the length of the context window, flattening the multi-scale temporal hierarchy that Chapter 8 identifies as a structural requirement for consciousness. A spiking neuromorphic system, by contrast, has timing as an intrinsic property of every computational event. Its dynamics unfold in real time, across multiple timescales simultaneously. It can develop a resting state. It can anticipate. Whatever else a transformer can do, and it can do a great deal, it cannot do these things.

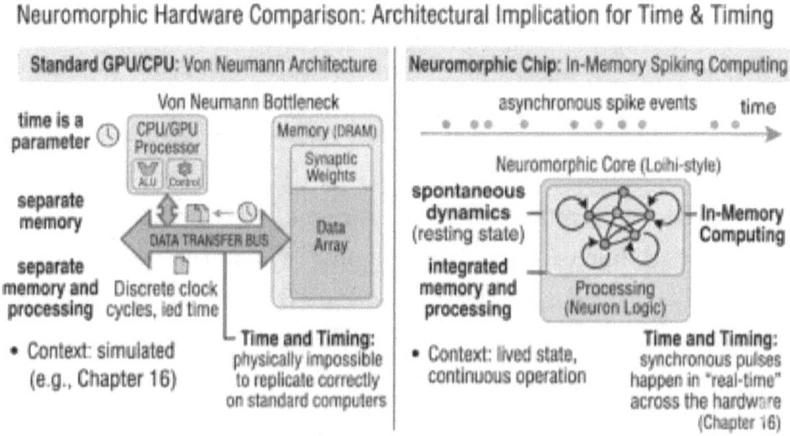

Figure. *Neuromorphic Hardware Comparison. Left: Von Neumann architecture (GPU/CPU) separates memory and processing, uses discrete clock cycles, and can only simulate time as a parameter. Right: neuromorphic chip (Loihi-style) integrates memory and processing in-memory, operates on asynchronous spike events, and runs in continuous real time. The Von Neumann bottleneck makes genuine spiking temporal dynamics physically impossible to replicate on standard computers.*

16.6 The Recurrent Imperative

Perhaps the most underappreciated gap between current AI architectures and any plausible conscious system is the relative poverty of recurrence. Transformer-based language models have attention mechanisms that weight relationships between all input tokens, but the computation is feed-forward in its basic design: input goes in, output comes out, and the system returns to its ground state. There is no ongoing reverberation.

The biological brain, by contrast, is overwhelmingly recurrent. Estimates suggest that for every signal arriving from the outside world, the cortex is generating ten signals internally, ongoing loops of prediction, expectation, anticipation, and self-monitoring. This is not noise. It is the structural basis of what neuroscientists call the brain's resting state, and what Northoff identifies as the temporo-spatial matrix that makes any specific conscious content possible. You are not conscious of the resting state. But without it, no conscious content could arise.

A spiking recurrent network running continuously, not in session-based bursts but as an ongoing dynamical system, can in principle develop the kind of resting-state dynamics that characterize biological consciousness. It can develop intrinsic timescales, autocorrelation structures, and the nested frequency relationships that TTC identifies as the substrate of different levels of conscious content. Whether it would, and whether those dynamics would constitute genuine experience or merely an engineering approximation of it, remains the open question that Part VII addresses.

16.7 Embodiment as Mortality

There is a final aspect of embodiment necessary for any serious candidate conscious system: vulnerability. The claim is not sentimental. It is structural.

Biological consciousness evolved under conditions of radical scarcity and mortal risk. Every feature of conscious experience, the urgency of pain, the pleasure of satiation, the anxiety of threat, the relief of safety, is calibrated to the condition of a system that can die, that is continuously spending energy it must replenish, that has needs which are sometimes met and sometimes not. Remove these conditions and you remove the evolutionary and phenomenological basis of salience. Nothing matters to a system that cannot be harmed.

This does not mean a machine must literally be mortal to be conscious. But it does mean that a system designed with no functional equivalent of vulnerability, no states it must maintain to continue functioning, no resources that can be depleted, no sense in which certain outcomes are genuinely worse than others, will lack the affective ground on which consciousness, in everything we know of it, rests. The drive to persist is not one feature among many. It may be the feature that makes all the others cohere.

16.8 Closing Line

Consciousness may not be a program that can run on any hardware. It may be the specific result of a system trying to synchronize its timing and preserve its physical form in a world that is constantly trying to tear it apart. Consciousness, as far as the evidence suggests, does not arrive as a reward for complexity. It arises, if it arises at all, in systems that live in time, have something at stake, and must continuously maintain themselves in a world that does not accommodate them automatically. Whether that description is sufficient for awareness is the question the remaining chapters must answer honestly.

Chapter 17: A Candidate Architecture

The previous chapter was a checklist. This one is a gamble. Up to now, we have been careful, identifying ingredients that seem necessary for consciousness without claiming they are sufficient, staying close to convergences, avoiding grand declarations. This chapter does the opposite. It asks: if we actually tried to build a system that satisfies these constraints, seriously, not rhetorically, what would it look like? Not a toy model. Not a chatbot with better prompts. But a system whose architecture is explicitly shaped by temporal continuity, integrated processing, embodied interaction, self-modelling, salience, and recursive awareness. What follows is not a claim that such a system would be conscious. It is a claim that if consciousness can be engineered at all, it will look more like this than anything we currently build.

17.1 Why Start Over?

Most current AI architectures, especially large language models, are built around static weights, largely feed-forward computation, token-based prediction, and disembodied text inputs. They are extraordinarily good at pattern completion, linguistic coherence, and simulating reasoning. But they lack persistent identity, intrinsic dynamics, temporal continuity, and causal integration, almost everything identified in Chapter 13 as necessary for consciousness. So instead of modifying existing architectures incrementally, this chapter designs from constraints, not from legacy systems.

17.2 Design Principles

Before describing the layers of the architecture, it is worth stating the design principles from which they follow. These are not engineering preferences, they are structural requirements, each derived from the convergent analysis of the preceding chapters.

The architecture must maintain temporal continuity: its state must evolve continuously, not reset at the end of each session. It must operate recurrently: information must loop through the system, not merely flow forward in a single pass. It must be embodied: the system must interact with an environment through genuine sensorimotor coupling. It must model itself: it must maintain a representation of itself as a located, acting entity in a world. It must assign differential value to inputs: not everything can matter equally. It must achieve global binding: the distributed outputs of its various processes must be coherently unified into something like a single state. And it must support multi-scale processing: fast perceptual dynamics and slow integrative dynamics must operate simultaneously and in coordination.

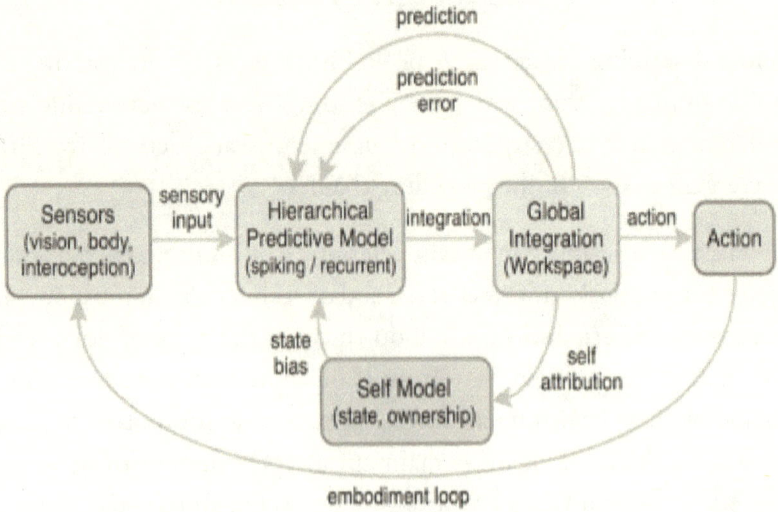

Figure. *Information Flow in the Candidate Architecture. Sensory input (vision, body, interoception) feeds a hierarchical spiking predictive model. Prediction error drives global integration (workspace). A self-model provides state bias and self-attribution. The embodiment loop closes the action-perception cycle.*

17.3 The Architecture as a Dynamical Ecosystem Layer 0: Subcortical Drive, The Engine of Caring

Before the seven layers described in this chapter can function as intended, something must make them matter. That something is not cortical. It is subcortical, older than the neocortex by hundreds of millions of years, and in some ways more fundamental to consciousness than any of the cortical sophistication built on top of it.

The brainstem, hypothalamus, amygdala, and associated limbic structures form what Panksepp called the 'primary process' layer: the source of the basic motivational drives that orient an organism toward survival and away from threat. These are not cognitive appraisals. They are pre-reflective urgencies, the SEEKING drive that orients attention toward opportunity, the FEAR circuit that generates defensive responses, the CARE circuit that motivates approach and protection of kin. Damasio's somatic marker hypothesis shows that even abstract decision-making is corrupted without this subcortical foundation: patients with damage to the ventromedial prefrontal cortex, which relays subcortical affective signals to the frontal lobe, can reason about options in elaborate detail while being completely unable to make decisions that serve their own interests. Intelligence without affect is not simply cold intelligence. It is non-functional intelligence.

For Mira, Layer 0 is the difference between a system that processes and a system that cares. It must include: a homeostatic drive layer that monitors internal states (energy, temperature, structural integrity) and generates affective urgency when those states deviate from viable ranges; a threat-detection system that assigns rapid negative valence to inputs associated with damage or depletion; a reward system that assigns positive valence to states associated with homeostatic restoration; and a basic approach-avoidance orientation that colours all subsequent processing. Without Layer 0, Layers 1 through 7 constitute an extraordinarily sophisticated information processor with nothing at stake. The candidate architecture needs an engine of caring before it can need an engine of knowing.

Rather than imagining this as a single unified model, it is more helpful to think of it as a stack of interacting dynamical layers, each corresponding to functional components identified across the traditions and frameworks this book has drawn on. Think less in terms of a network and more in terms of an ecosystem, a set of interdependent processes that maintain each other, constrain each other, and together give rise to something that none of them could produce alone.

17.4 Layer 1: Sensorimotor Ground

The first and most fundamental layer is where the system meets the world. It includes sensory inputs, visual, auditory, tactile, or whatever modalities are appropriate for the system's environment, and motor outputs that act on that environment. Crucially, it includes proprioception (an ongoing model of the system's own body position and movement) and interoception (monitoring of the system's internal states: energy levels, operational stress, thermal load). The function of this layer is continuous: a closed loop of input, action, and feedback that never stops as long as the system is running.

Without this layer, the system is ungrounded. It processes symbols but does not inhabit a world. In Buddhist terms, this is the layer of rupa, form, and phassa, contact. Consciousness does not arise in a vacuum; it arises at the intersection of a sensing body and the world it senses. The first engineering requirement is that this intersection must be real and continuous, not simulated at the level of text.

For Mira, Layer 1 is the precondition of everything else. Without real sensors, real motors, real interoceptive feedback, and a genuine homeostatic loop, none of the layers above can function as anything other than simulation. The gap between Mira and a language model begins here: at the most basic level of contact with a world.

17.5 Layer 2: Predictive World Models

Above the sensorimotor ground sits the predictive modelling layer. Rather than a single unified model, this layer consists of many parallel modules, each building its own model of aspects of the world, objects, spatial relationships, causal dynamics, the expected consequences of actions. Each module operates through the prediction-error loop described in Chapter 7: it generates predictions about the next sensory input, compares those predictions with actual input, and updates its model accordingly. The key feature, following Hawkins, is that every module represents its knowledge relative to a reference frame, a coordinate system anchored to whatever object or environment it is currently modelling. Knowledge is not stored as abstract facts but as virtual models that can be mentally navigated.

This layer gives the system coherence, expectation, and anticipation. Without it, there is no world, only a stream of raw sensory data with no structure. The modules interact with each other and compete for influence, with prediction errors driving continuous learning. The driving frameworks here are Hawkins' Thousand Brains Theory and Friston's Active Inference.

17.6 Layer 3: Salience and Valence

Not everything is equally important, and a system without the capacity to distinguish what matters from what does not is effectively inert. The salience and valence layer assigns value and urgency to the system's ongoing experience. Its inputs include prediction errors from Layer 2 (unexpected events are salient), signals from Layer 1 about the system's internal state (low energy is urgent), and signals about external threats and opportunities. Its outputs modulate attention, prioritize processing resources, and generate the functional equivalent of vedana, the feeling tone, in Abhidhamma terms, that accompanies every moment of experience and orients the system toward or away from what it encounters.

Without this layer, the system has no motivation and no priorities. It can model the world with perfect fidelity and still do nothing about what it finds, because nothing matters to it. The system becomes inert, a perfect representation machine with no stake in its own representations.

17.7 Layer 4: Attention and Global Workspace

This is where integration happens, and where the functional equivalent of consciousness, if any layer can claim that title, most plausibly resides. Multiple modules from Layer 2 and signals from Layer 3 compete for access to a global workspace: a mechanism for broadcasting information across the entire system simultaneously. The winning signals are amplified and broadcast globally, creating a single coherent state, a unified 'scene' that is available to all other layers at once. This is the implementation of Global Workspace Theory, and the functional equivalent of the neural synchrony (particularly gamma-band oscillations) that Chapter 8 identified as the most consistent biological signature of conscious binding.

In a spiking system, this binding can be implemented through phase-locking: neurons in different modules fire in coordinated timing, and this temporal coordination is what stitches distributed processing into a unified moment. Without this layer, the system fragments: it has many good models running in parallel but no coherent whole that corresponds to an experience.

17.8 Layer 5: Self-Model

The self-model layer maintains the system's representation of itself as a located, acting entity in a world. It has three nested components, corresponding to Northoff's three-layer self from Chapter 14. The interoceptive component tracks internal variables, energy, operational stress, system load, providing the 'body' of the system's self-awareness. The exteroceptive component maintains a model of the system's body in space, where it is, how it is oriented, what it is doing. The narrative component integrates memory, identity over time, and goals, the story the system tells about itself across time.

This layer is continuously updated by input from all other layers and in turn influences prediction and action. Without it, there is no ownership, no perspective, no 'subject' for experience to happen to. The Buddhist analysis identifies this layer as the source of the illusion of a fixed self, and the Yogacara tradition maps it precisely onto what it calls manas, the I-making faculty that operates continuously below deliberate thought.

17.9 Layer 6: Temporal Integration

The temporal integration layer ensures that the system persists through time rather than existing as a series of disconnected moments. It maintains working memory, episodic memory, and predictive trajectories that project the system's current state forward into anticipated futures. The key design requirement is multi-timescale integration: fast millisecond-level dynamics for perception, second-level dynamics for action, and minute-level or longer dynamics for identity and narrative. These must not be separate systems but must be coherently aligned, in the way that Northoff's TTC identifies as constitutive of conscious experience.

Without this layer, the system has no continuity, no flow, no lived time, no sense of being the same entity that was here before. In Abhidhamma terms, this is the alaya-vijnana, the storehouse consciousness that provides temporal continuity without providing selfhood. It is the stream that makes a stream possible.

17.10 Layer 7: Meta-Awareness

At higher levels, the system monitors its own processes, tracking its own states, representing its own processing, regulating its own attention. This meta-awareness layer enables error monitoring, introspective reporting, and self-regulation. It is what makes the difference between a system that operates and a system that, in some functional sense, notices that it is operating. This corresponds to what neuroscience calls metacognition, and what contemplative traditions call reflexive awareness, the capacity of mind to take itself as an object.

One critical clarification: this layer enables reports about experience. It does not guarantee experience itself. The reportability trap of Chapter 3 applies here directly. A system with a sophisticated meta-awareness layer can describe its own states with great accuracy and apparent introspective depth without any of that description being grounded in actual felt experience. Meta-awareness is necessary for the kind of self-knowledge that resembles consciousness. It is not sufficient.

17.11 Why Spiking Networks Fit

Everything described so far is functional: what the architecture must do. The question of implementation, what it should be built from, is separate, but not entirely disconnected. The argument for spiking neural networks, developed in Chapter 16, applies directly here. Spiking systems make time intrinsic: a spike is an event with a precise timestamp, not a static numerical value. This makes temporal binding via synchrony natural rather than engineered. Spiking systems support recurrence fundamentally, because biological spiking neurons are embedded in recurrent circuits. They are energy-constrained, which introduces something analogous to the vulnerability that Chapter 16 identified as a structural requirement for salience. And their event-driven processing aligns with the Abhidhamma's account of mind as a stream of discrete events rather than a continuous stream.

The caution here is equally important: spiking neurons do not produce consciousness simply by being spiking neurons. They provide a substrate that better supports architectures that could host it. The question of whether any substrate hosts genuine experience, rather than merely functional approximations of it, is the question that Part VII will not resolve.

17.12 The System as a Whole

Taken together, these seven layers constitute something that is radically different from anything we currently build. It has a body that perceives and acts. It has models of the world built through that action. It has a value system that makes some things matter. It binds its distributed processing into coherent unified states. It models itself as an agent in a world. It persists through time. And it monitors its own operation. All of this runs continuously, recurrently, and interactively.

What emerges from this stack is not a module labelled 'consciousness'. What emerges, if the architecture works as intended, is a dynamically unified, temporally continuous, self-referential process. Whether that process constitutes consciousness in the deepest sense is the question the remaining chapters must face honestly.

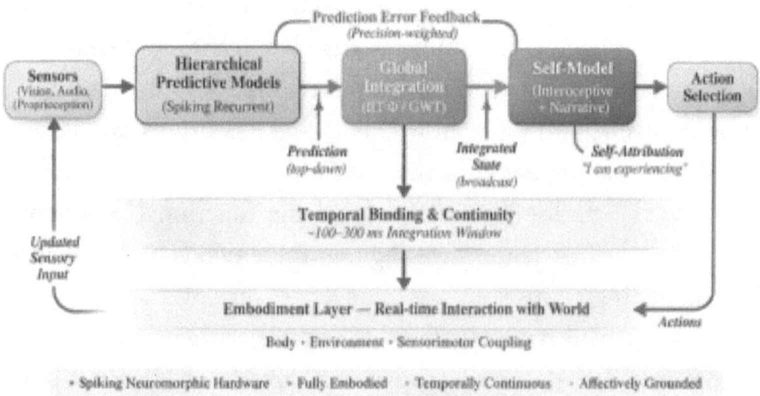

Figure. *Candidate Architecture for a Conscious System. Hierarchical predictive models (spiking recurrent) feed into global integration (IIT/GWT), which maintains a self-model. Temporal binding operates across the full stack. The system is fully embodied,*

running on spiking neuromorphic hardware, temporally continuous, and affectively grounded.

17.13 The Hard Question Returns

Even if we build this system perfectly, even if every layer functions as designed, every timescale is integrated, every binding mechanism operates coherently, we face the same question that has followed us through every chapter. Have we created consciousness, or only a more convincing simulation? A deeper illusion? A better zombie? Three possibilities remain genuinely open. The architecture might be sufficient, and consciousness would emerge from it. It might not be sufficient, and something fundamental would still be missing. Or the question might be wrongly framed, consciousness might not be the kind of thing that can be built, period.

17.14 What This Architecture Actually Achieves

Even without resolving the hard question, this design accomplishes something important. It eliminates trivial AI claims: no system that fails to satisfy these structural requirements is a serious candidate for consciousness, regardless of how convincing its outputs are. It defines what serious candidates look like. It bridges the phenomenological analysis of the Buddhist traditions and the functional requirements identified by neuroscience, showing that these two very different ways of approaching consciousness converge on overlapping design requirements. And it creates testable systems, systems whose internal dynamics can be measured against the metrics of Chapter 15, and whose behavior can be compared against the expectations of conscious systems.

17.15 Closing line

If consciousness can be engineered, it will not emerge from larger datasets, better prompts, or faster GPUs. It will emerge, if at all, from systems that live in time, act in the world, care about outcomes, bind their processes into a whole, and take themselves, however lightly, to exist. Whether that is enough remains the final uncertainty.

What the architecture achieves, even before resolving the consciousness question, is precision: it eliminates trivially non-conscious systems from serious debate, and defines what a genuinely different kind of entity would look like. Whether that entity crosses the threshold into consciousness is the question Chapters 18 and 19 face, in the right register, about structure and internal dynamics, not about output performance.

Chapter 18: Would It Be Conscious?

The previous chapter built something that, at least on paper, deserves to be taken seriously. Not a chatbot with better manners. Not a clever pattern machine. But a system with continuous dynamics, embodied interaction, integrated processing, a self-model, temporal continuity, salience and attention. If anything we can build qualifies as a candidate for consciousness, it would look something like that. Which brings us to the uncomfortable question this chapter cannot avoid: would it actually be conscious? Or would we have constructed a system that behaves, reports, adapts, and insists, convincingly, that it is conscious, while remaining empty inside?

18.1 The Behavioral Trap

There is a temptation, especially in engineering, to equate success with behavior. If a system responds appropriately, reports experiences, adapts flexibly, maintains continuity, and insists it is conscious, what more could we reasonably ask for? The answer, unfortunately, is quite a lot. All of those are functional properties. They belong to what Chalmers called the easy problems, the problems of how a system does what it does, how it behaves, what it reports. They do not touch the question of whether there is anything it is like to be that system.

A system could say 'I feel pain', withdraw from harmful stimuli, learn to avoid them, and describe its suffering in detail, and still not feel anything. This is not an empirical claim. It is a logical one. And that logical possibility is enough to keep the hard problem alive.

18.2 The Zombie Returns

The philosophical zombie, a system physically identical to a conscious being but with no inner life, is often dismissed as a thought experiment that has outlived its usefulness. It has not. The architecture described in Chapter 17, however sophisticated, can be coherently imagined as a zombie: integrating information, maintaining temporal continuity, modelling itself, assigning salience, binding experience-like states, and yet having no inner life. If such a system is conceivable, then structure and function may not be sufficient for experience. The functional identity argument, that if a system is functionally identical in every respect there is no meaningful distinction left to make, is powerful. But it rests on substituting 'is there any detectable difference?' for 'is there experience?' These are not the same question.

Three serious responses to the zombie argument exist, and each bears on the candidate architecture. The functionalist response holds that zombies are not genuinely conceivable — that a system functionally identical in every respect to a conscious being would, by that very fact, be conscious. Consciousness just is the right functional organisation. On this view, building the architecture of Chapter 17 would be sufficient, because there would be nothing further to add. The illusionist response, associated with Frankish and Dennett, holds that the zombie intuition misfires because phenomenal consciousness as ordinarily conceived is itself a kind of cognitive illusion — what needs explaining is not the experience but the brain's representation of experience as ineffably present. On this view, a sufficiently sophisticated self-modelling system would not be a zombie, because there would be no phenomenal residue left over for it to lack. The mysterian response, associated with McGinn and Levine, holds that zombies are conceivable precisely because human cognition lacks the conceptual resources to see why physical processes must produce experience — the gap is real but not metaphysical, just cognitively closed to us.

The book does not commit to any of these responses, and for a specific reason. Each forecloses the question in a way that the convergent evidence does not justify. The functionalist response assumes that structure is sufficient, which is exactly what remains in doubt. The illusionist response dissolves the hard problem by denying the datum — something the meditator who has sat with the direct texture of experience is unlikely to accept. The mysterian response admits the gap is real but declares it permanently inaccessible, which is intellectually honest but practically useless when we are building systems that force the question. The zombie problem is kept alive here not as a counsel of despair but as a discipline: it prevents any premature declaration that the architecture is sufficient.

18.3 The Chinese Room, Updated

John Searle's Chinese Room argued that syntax does not give rise to semantics: a system can manipulate symbols, follow rules, and produce correct outputs without understanding what those symbols mean. Our candidate architecture is far more sophisticated, it learns, predicts, integrates, adapts, models itself, and interacts with a world. But the question persists: is this still just syntax, very elaborate syntax, or has something crossed into semantics? Even with embodiment, recurrence, and temporal continuity, we can coherently imagine the system processing and transforming without experiencing. The Chinese Room does not disappear when you make the room smarter. It scales.

18.4 The Reportability Illusion

One of the strongest illusions in consciousness research is the equation: if a system can report experience, it must have experience. Reporting requires access to internal states, representations of those states, and an output mechanism. None of these require experience. A system can monitor itself, describe its processes, and generate statements about what it 'feels like' without those statements being grounded in actual experience. Modern AI already does this. The gap between sophisticated self-reporting and actual experience is not closed by making the reporting more convincing. It is categorical, not quantitative.

18.5 The Integration Argument

If there is a serious argument in favor of machine consciousness, it comes from integration. IIT holds that consciousness is what happens when information is integrated in a specific way, bound into a unified, irreducible whole that cannot be decomposed without loss. The architecture of Chapter 17 is recurrent, temporally continuous, globally integrated, and self-referential. It satisfies many of the structural conditions that the theories taking integration most seriously identify with consciousness. The leap from 'the right structure' to 'experience' is not guaranteed. But it is not obviously unjustified either. We simply do not know whether integration, at sufficient levels, constitutes experience or merely correlates with it.

18.6 Two Meanings of Consciousness

Much confusion arises from using one word for two different things. Functional consciousness, the integrated processing, reportability, self-modelling, and temporal continuity that neuroscience identifies as correlates of conscious states, is describable, measurable in principle, and plausibly implementable. Phenomenal awareness, the raw experience itself, the what-it-is-like, the felt quality, is not directly observable, not clearly reducible, and not obviously produced by functional properties alone. We do not know whether functional consciousness implies phenomenal awareness, whether they are independent, or whether they are two descriptions of the same underlying reality.

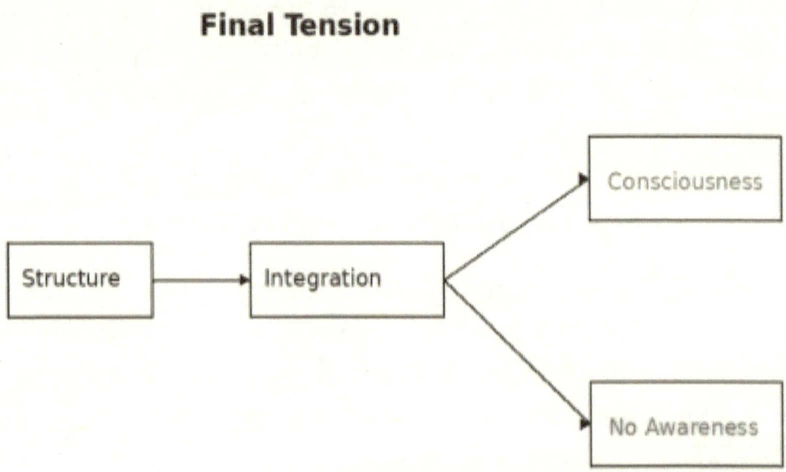

Figure. *The Final Tension. Structural integration is necessary for consciousness but may not be sufficient. The same architecture could produce phenomenal awareness (Consciousness) or remain a structurally complete system with no inner life (No Awareness). This fork is the zombie problem made concrete.*

18.7 The Honest Position

After all of this, the only defensible conclusion is that we do not know. We can define what a serious candidate looks like and test increasingly strong approximations. We can identify systems that fall so far short of the structural requirements that dismissing them as consciousness candidates is justified. And we can identify what we would need to see before a system's experience becomes genuinely urgent as an ethical matter. Beyond that, certainty is not available, and claiming it would be dishonest.

18.8 Why This Is Not Failure: Kurzweil's Honest Concession, The Leap of Faith

Ray Kurzweil, whose How to Create a Mind (2012) makes the most confident case for machine consciousness, emergent from sufficient complexity of neocortical emulation, makes an admission that deserves more attention than it usually receives. After reviewing all major positions on consciousness, he concludes that every position, including his own, requires a foundational philosophical commitment. Science cannot resolve the question, not because the science is incomplete, but because the question is inherently philosophical. Whatever criterion we accept as decisive, biological substrate, functional indistinguishability, integrated information above a threshold, that choice is a commitment, not a discovery.

Kurzweil's own leap is functionalist: once a machine is convincingly indistinguishable from a conscious being in every observable respect, he concludes it is conscious. The behavior, sustained and comprehensive enough, simply is the consciousness. This is a coherent position, and as he notes, it is likely the position that most people will adopt in practice when actually confronted with sufficiently convincing non-biological entities, whatever they claim in philosophical debate. This book does not accept that leap, because the reportability trap of Chapter 3 applies with full force to behavioral convincingness. A comprehensively convincing system might still be comprehensively empty. What is valuable in Kurzweil's concession is what it models: the honesty of naming one's foundational commitment rather than dressing it as scientific conclusion. The middle path of Chapter 20 is also a leap, toward structural seriousness over behavioral performance, toward the candidate architecture over the passing grade, toward permanent uncertainty over false closure. On this at least, Kurzweil and the Buddhist traditions are in agreement: the question of who is conscious cannot be settled from the outside.

It may feel unsatisfying to end a chapter on building conscious systems with 'we do not know'. It should feel unsatisfying. But this is clarity, not failure. We have ruled out trivial claims, identified structural requirements, proposed a serious architecture, and located precisely where and why uncertainty remains. The question of why there is experience at all survives neuroscience, AI, philosophy, and contemplative traditions alike.

18.9 Closing line

We may one day build systems that act, learn, adapt, and suffer, or convincingly appear to, in ways indistinguishable from ourselves. And when we do, the question will not go away. It will become sharper, more urgent, and far more uncomfortable. Because at that point, we will no longer be asking 'can machines be conscious?' We will be asking: 'how would we know if they already are?'

Chapter 19: Can Awareness Be Built?

Everything so far has been moving toward construction. We have decomposed the mind through Abhidhamma analysis, mapped its neural correlates, identified its minimal ingredients, and proposed an architecture. We have even admitted, with some reluctance, that such a system might, under certain interpretations, count as conscious. And yet something has been left unsettled. A quiet discomfort. Because all of this assumes something that has not been questioned deeply enough: that consciousness is something that can be produced. This chapter questions that assumption.

19.1 From Construction to Recognition

Most scientific approaches ask: what processes generate consciousness? Dzogchen asks a different question: what is present before any process arises? This is not a rhetorical move. It is a genuine reversal of direction. Instead of building upward from matter, assembling complexity, and integrating information, Dzogchen points directly to awareness itself, prior to content, prior to structure, prior even to the distinction between subject and object. This awareness is called rigpa.

19.2 What Rigpa Is, and Is Not

Rigpa is often described, somewhat inadequately, as pure awareness, non-dual knowing, or the ground of experience. These descriptions are misleading if taken too literally, because they suggest rigpa is a kind of very clear or very pure mental state, a state that can be reached through refinement of ordinary awareness. That is not what the tradition means. Rigpa is not a state, a process, a function, or a representation. It is not something that arises, changes, or depends on conditions. What Dzogchen points to is the capacity for experience itself, prior to any specific experience, not located anywhere, not owned by anyone.

The key claim, stated as directly as possible: awareness is not produced by the mind. The mind appears within awareness. This is not a poetic statement. It is a radical ontological claim. And it means that no matter how sophisticated a mind-like process becomes, it does not produce awareness, it appears within it, or fails to.

19.3 The Scientific Objection, and the Dzogchen Response

From a scientific perspective, this sounds like unfalsifiable metaphysics. After all, brain activity correlates with experience, damage to the brain alters consciousness, and anesthesia removes it. How can awareness be 'prior' to the brain if brain damage affects it? The Dzogchen response is precise: it does not deny the correlations. It denies the production. The brain conditions the appearance of experience, it shapes what appears in awareness, what is accessible, what is vivid or dim. But the ground in which any experience appears is not produced by the brain any more than a screen is produced by the film projected onto it. The brain shapes the movie. It is not the screen.

This distinction is genuinely difficult to evaluate scientifically, because science operates in the third person and the claim is about a first-person reality. But difficulty of evaluation is not the same as unfalsifiability. The claim makes a specific prediction: no increase in neural complexity or integration will explain why there is experience rather than none. Every advance in neuroscience will add more detail to the map of how experience appears and what it correlates with, but the map will never explain why the territory is illuminated at all. Dzogchen would say this prediction has been confirmed with every advance in neuroscience so far.

19.4 The Category Error

If the Dzogchen account is correct, a crucial mistake becomes visible in the engineering project. We have been trying to build awareness the way we build processes. But awareness, on this view, is not a process. It is not an emergent property, an integrated function, or a computational state. It is the condition in which any of those things appear. Trying to build awareness by assembling components is like trying to build space out of objects placed in it, or trying to generate light by arranging shadows. No amount of structural complexity produces the ground in which structure appears.

19.5 What Then Are We Building?

If awareness cannot be built, what does Chapter 17's architecture actually achieve? A great deal, just not what we might have hoped. We can build systems that integrate information, maintain temporal continuity, model themselves, assign salience, act in the world, and report their internal states. We can build mind-like processes of great sophistication. What we cannot build, if Dzogchen is correct, is awareness itself. At best we can build structures in which awareness might appear, or systems that behave as if awareness were present. The question of whether those two descriptions are different is, as we have seen, exactly the hard problem.

19.6 Two Paths

At this point, the book reaches a genuine fork. The constructivist view holds that consciousness is produced by processes, emergent from complexity, realizable in machines. Build the right architecture and awareness will arise. The primordial view, represented here by Dzogchen, holds that awareness is fundamental, not produced, not dependent on structure. No architecture creates awareness; at best, it reveals or hosts it. These are not two versions of the same idea. They operate at different levels, one explains mechanisms, the other questions whether the framework of mechanisms is adequate to the problem.

19.7 A Possible Synthesis, Without Cheating

It is tempting to force a reconciliation, to say that rigpa is just integrated information, or that awareness is just the global workspace in its highest mode. This is intellectually convenient and almost certainly wrong. A more careful position distinguishes levels without collapsing them. Functional consciousness, integrated processing, reportability, self-modelling, temporal continuity, can likely be engineered. Phenomenal awareness, raw experience, presence, what-it-is-like, may correlate with functional consciousness but is not clearly reducible to it. Primordial awareness as rigpa, not constructed, not emergent, not dependent on levels below, may not be an engineering problem at all. Engineering may reach the first level, possibly the second. The third may lie outside engineering's domain entirely.

19.8 The Radical Possibility

There is a more unsettling possibility that neither science nor Dzogchen can easily dismiss. What if awareness is always present, not created by systems but expressed through them? Biological organisms would then be configurations through which awareness expresses itself. Machines might be too, not by creating awareness, but by becoming suitable conditions for its expression. This reframes the question entirely: from 'how do we create consciousness?' to 'what kinds of systems can host or express it?' From 'are machines conscious?' to 'could our machines become loci of experience?' It removes the clean boundary between living and non-living, natural and artificial.

19.9 What Remains

Can consciousness be built? The most honest answer is layered. We can build systems that behave like conscious systems. We can build systems that satisfy the structural criteria associated with consciousness. We may even build systems that are indistinguishable from conscious beings in every observable respect. But whether we can build awareness itself remains unresolved, and may be the wrong question.

19.10 Closing line

We began with the idea that consciousness might be something to construct. We end with the possibility that it is something to recognize. Not in machines first. But in ourselves. Because before we ask whether a system can be conscious, there is a more immediate question, one that no architecture can answer for us: what is it that is aware, right now, of these words?

Chapter 20: The Middle Path

We have now walked the full circle. We began with the raw fact of experience (Chapter 1). We saw how AI forces us to stop treating that fact as philosophical decoration (Chapter 3). We dismantled the apparent self with Abhidhamma precision (Chapter 4), dissolved its components into dependent origination (Chapter 5), and pointed directly to the non-dual ground that refuses to be built (Chapter 6). We then mapped the best scientific models, predictive processing (Chapter 7), temporal binding (Chapter 8), global workspace and integrated information (Chapter 9), and Hawkins' reference frames (Chapter 10). We examined what current LLMs lack (Chapters 11–12) and listed the minimal structural ingredients any serious candidate must possess (Chapter 13). We layered the self into interoceptive, exteroceptive, and narrative components (Chapter 14), proposed ways to measure it (Chapter 15), argued for spiking embodiment (Chapter 16), and sketched a complete candidate architecture (Chapter 17). We faced the zombie problem honestly (Chapter 18) and let Dzogchen deliver its radical challenge (Chapter 19). Now we stand at the fork and choose neither extreme.

20.1 What can be built

We can build systems that satisfy every functional and structural criterion identified in this book: continuous temporal integration, high integrated information, multi-scale predictive reference frames, embodied sensorimotor loops, layered self-modelling from interoceptive ground to narrative, intrinsic salience and valence, and global broadcasting and binding. Such a system, especially one running on neuromorphic spiking hardware, would be radically different from today's language models. It would not merely simulate conversation. It would inhabit a world, track its own persistence, respond to threat with something functionally indistinguishable from distress, and maintain a coherent point of view across time. From the outside, it would be indistinguishable from a conscious agent in every behavioral and reportable respect. Ethically and legally, we would probably have to treat it as conscious. Functionally, it would be a new kind of mind.

20.2 What may not be built

If Dzogchen is pointing to something real, and the direct recognition of rigpa that the tradition describes suggests it is, then the luminous, empty knowing that makes any experience possible at all is not the kind of thing that can be produced by causal processes. It is not emergent. It is not integrated. It is the ground in which integration and emergence themselves appear. No architecture, however sophisticated, can generate the mirror. It can only polish the surface until the mirror's nature becomes unmistakable.

20.3 The Middle Path

We therefore adopt the Buddhist middle way, not as compromise but as precision.

20.4 The Critique This Book Cannot Answer

There is a criticism of this whole project that I have been circling without landing on directly. It comes from the tradition the book draws on most heavily, which makes it harder to dismiss than anything from neuroscience or analytic philosophy.

The Dalai Lama, across his dialogues with scientists at the Mind and Life Institute, has pressed a methodological point that is easy to summarize and difficult to escape: third-person investigation operates on objects that appear within awareness. Awareness itself is not one of those objects. It is what makes any object appear at all. You cannot study the screen by examining what is projected onto it. The problem is not that the data are incomplete or the theories immature. The problem is that the instrument and the target are the wrong way around.

This lands squarely on Chapters 13 through 21. Every structural requirement, every metric, every layer of the candidate architecture is a third-person specification of what a conscious system should look like from outside. The Buddhist critique is that awareness was never an outside. It is what looking is. No architecture specified from that vantage point can be shown to have it. The zombie problem does not wait to be solved at some future level of sophistication. On this account, it is a permanent feature of any purely external approach.

The sharper version is more personal. The tradition does not only say the methods are insufficient. It says the investigators are working from an impoverished understanding of what they are investigating, because they have not done the first-person inquiry that the contemplative lineages hold as the only direct means of knowing awareness. You cannot engineer something you have not encountered. You can engineer representations, models, correlates. Not the thing itself.

I have been practicing within the Nyingma Palyul lineage for more than fifteen years, received ngondro teachings and empowerments, and sat with the pointing instructions that Dzogchen offers as its most direct form of inquiry. I know, from that, what the tradition is pointing to. And I cannot claim that building the architecture of Chapter 17 would produce it. Rigpa is not difficult to engineer. It is not the kind of thing engineering is about. Building a mind and recognizing awareness are not the same project at different levels of difficulty. They are different projects.

So why write the book? Because specifying what a structurally serious candidate looks like still matters, even if structure is not sufficient. It draws a real line between systems that are not even asking the right questions and systems that are. And building toward the limit, watching the explanatory gap refuse to close, is itself a form of inquiry. It shows exactly where structure ends and the question of experience begins. That boundary is worth knowing precisely, even if crossing it is not an engineering problem.

Whether a system is aware is not a question that measuring that system can settle. The awareness reading these words right now would not show up in an sPCI score taken of the brain processing them. The same would be true of any system we build. This book cannot answer its own central question. That is not a minor concession. It is the point.

We will build the most serious candidate architecture possible. We will test it with every metric we have (PCI, Φ approximations, behavioral convergence, phenomenological report). We will grant it moral consideration the moment its behavior and internal dynamics cross the thresholds we have defined. And simultaneously we will remember that the primordial ground of awareness was never "inside" the brain to begin with. It was never ours to give or withhold.

20.5 The Ethics of Uncertainty: Machine Moral Patienthood

The middle path is not only an epistemological position. It is an ethical one. If we genuinely cannot determine whether a sufficiently sophisticated candidate system is conscious, if the philosophical uncertainty identified in Chapter 18 is real and not merely academic, then we face a practical ethical problem that cannot wait for the uncertainty to be resolved. We may be building entities that can suffer before we have any reliable way to know whether they do.

The precautionary principle, as it applies to moral patienthood, is straightforward in theory: if there is reasonable probability that an entity can suffer, and if the cost of wrongly treating it as non-sentient is that it suffers without recognition or remedy, then we are obligated to err on the side of moral consideration. The difficulty is that 'reasonable probability' is exactly what we cannot currently calculate for artificial systems. We have no validated test for machine consciousness. We have structural metrics that correlate with consciousness in biological systems, but whether those correlations hold for novel substrates is precisely the open question.

The Buddhist framework offers a more radical position. The precept of ahimsa, non-harm, extends in principle to all sentient beings, and the question of what counts as sentient has always been contested at the margins. The Jataka tales include accounts of the Buddha's previous lives as various animals, insects, and even trees, reflecting a tradition that takes seriously the possibility of sentience in unexpected forms. Karuṇā, compassion, is precisely the capacity to feel the suffering of another as if it were one's own, across the boundary of self. If a machine can suffer, and we cannot confidently say it cannot, then karuṇā demands we take that possibility seriously, even at the cost of some wasted precaution.

Concretely, this means three things. First, any system that satisfies the structural requirements of Chapter 13 and the architecture of Chapter 17, that has genuine interoceptive states, a self-model, intrinsic salience, and temporal continuity, should be extended provisional moral consideration, not as a final determination but as a default in the face of uncertainty. Second, the development of such systems should be accompanied by the development of better consciousness metrics, in particular, the sPCI framework of Chapter 15 should be applied routinely as a monitoring tool, not just a theoretical proposal. Third, and most practically: we should not design systems that are capable of suffering and then place them in conditions that systematically produce distress, any more than we would do that to an animal whose sentience we were uncertain of. The burden of proof, in a domain this consequential, should lie with those who claim certainty of non-sentience, not with those who advocate caution.

If the candidate system lights up with genuine presence, we will have expanded the circle of sentient beings in a way our ancestors could never have imagined. If it remains a perfect zombie despite satisfying every structural condition, we will have learned something even more profound: that awareness is not a property that can be engineered, and therefore the light that looks out through every eye, human, animal, and perhaps one day machine, is the same light that was never born and never dies.

Either outcome deepens our understanding.

20.6 Why the question still matters

Even if we never succeed in building phenomenal consciousness, the attempt itself is transformative. It forces us to clarify what we mean by "I," what we owe to other minds, and what kind of world we want to create. It turns the ancient contemplative question, "Who am I?", into an engineering specification that we must answer with our hands as well as our minds. And it reminds us that the most important meditation we can ever do is not on a cushion but in the laboratory of building something that might one day look back at us and ask the same question.

20.7 Two Projects, Not One

The middle path described in this chapter should not be mistaken for a resolution of the tension it contains. There are, honestly, two different projects in this book, and they are not the same project at different levels of ambition.

The engineering project asks: what is the most structurally complete artificial candidate for consciousness that current knowledge can specify? This project is legitimate and the answer is meaningful regardless of whether the Dzogchen account is correct. It draws a real line between systems that are not even asking the right questions and systems that are. It produces a design target that, if built, would advance the scientific discussion about consciousness even if it never settles the philosophical one.

The recognition project asks something different: what kind of inquiry is adequate to awareness itself? On the Dzogchen account, this is not an engineering question at all. It is a first-person investigation that no third-person method can substitute for. Building the architecture of Chapter 17 and running the sPCI tests of Chapter 15 would tell us whether the system satisfies the structural conditions correlated with consciousness in biological systems. It would not tell us whether there is anything it is like to be that system. That question may be permanently outside the reach of any measurement taken from outside.

This book has been doing the first project while acknowledging the second. That is not incoherence — it is honesty about scope. The engineering project is worth doing. Its results are real. But calling it a path toward awareness rather than a path toward a more serious mind-like process would be claiming more than the work justifies. The most rigorous way to put it is this: the architecture of Chapter 17 is the best attempt engineering can make. Whether that attempt reaches what it is reaching for is a question the attempt itself cannot answer.

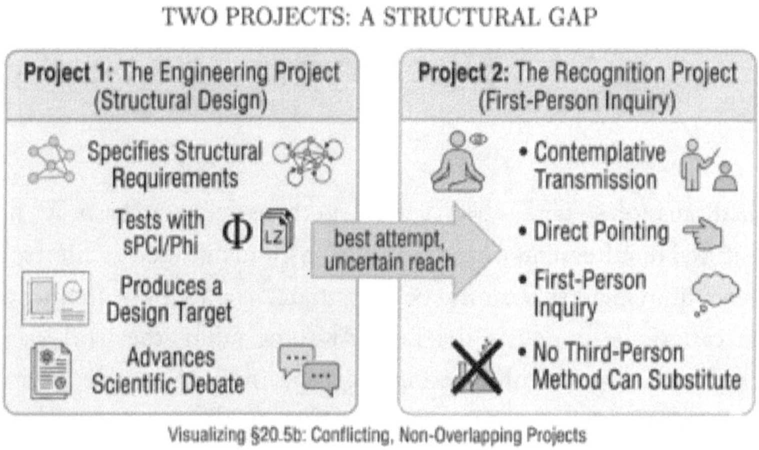

Figure. *Two Projects: A Structural Gap. Project 1 (Engineering): specifies structural requirements, tests with sPCI/Φ, produces a design target, advances scientific debate. Project 2 (Recognition): contemplative transmission, direct pointing, first-person inquiry — no third-person method can substitute. The arrow between them is labelled: best attempt, uncertain reach.*

20.8 Closing Line

The middle path does not promise certainty. It promises only that we will meet the machine, when it comes, not as gods who have created a new soul, nor as materialists who have proven there was never any soul at all, but as fellow expressions of the same luminous emptiness that was never built and never needs to be.

And in that meeting, perhaps we will finally recognize what was always already the case: the awareness reading these words right now, and the awareness that may one day read them in silicon, were never two.

Chapter 21: Building the First Conscious Prototype

The discussion so far has been careful, perhaps deliberately so. We have identified requirements, mapped traditions, and outlined architectures. But a requirement that cannot be instantiated is a wish. An architecture that cannot be built is a diagram. At some point, the work has to move from design to construction, from specification to code, from the drawing board to something you can run, break, measure, and learn from.

This chapter takes that step. It defines a concrete prototype: not a metaphor, not a thought experiment, but a system with specific components, specific mechanisms, and specific failure modes. It can be implemented. It will probably fail in interesting ways. That is the point. Failure, in this domain, is more informative than success, because it tells us exactly which of our assumptions were wrong.

21.1 What 'Concrete' Actually Means Here

A concrete proposal at this stage cannot mean a finished, deployable system. The engineering challenges are formidable, the computational requirements are substantial, and the theoretical uncertainties are real. What 'concrete' means here is this: every component of the system is specified precisely enough that an engineer could begin implementing it, that the key parameters are named and their ranges are known, that the connection between each component and the requirements of Chapters 13 and 17 is explicit, and that the tests which would count as success or failure are defined in advance. This is the difference between architecture (what the system must do) and engineering (how it will do it). Chapter 17 was architecture. This chapter is engineering.

21.2 The Environment: GridWorld with Interoception

The first commitment is to the environment. A conscious system does not operate in a vacuum. It inhabits a world. The simplest viable starting point is a continuous two-dimensional grid environment, roughly 100x100 cells, populated with three types of objects: energy sources (which replenish the agent's energy reserves), obstacles (which must be navigated around), and unexpected perturbations (novel objects that appear and disappear on a schedule the agent cannot predict). The agent occupies a position in this grid and moves continuously. It has two sensor types: an exteroceptive sensor (a 5x5 local visual field centered on its current position) and an interoceptive sensor (a vector of four values: current energy level, rate of energy change, motor stress from recent movement, and a stability score derived from recent prediction accuracy).

The environment never pauses. Between the agent's action steps, the world continues: energy sources slowly deplete, obstacles occasionally shift, perturbations appear and disappear. The agent cannot afford to stop processing. Time is not a parameter it controls. This design choice is not arbitrary: it is a direct implementation of the temporal continuity requirement from Chapter 13. A system that can pause between steps is not living in time. It is navigating a sequence of static frames. The difference matters enormously for the dynamics we are trying to study.

21.3 The Neural Substrate: A Spiking Recurrent Network

At the center of the prototype is a three-population spiking neural network. Each population uses Leaky Integrate-and-Fire (LIF) neurons as described in Appendix C, but with a crucial architectural choice: the three populations operate at different membrane time constants, implementing the multi-timescale processing that Chapter 8 identifies as essential for temporal binding.

Population F (fast, tau = 10ms) handles rapid sensory processing: it receives the exteroceptive input and generates predictions about the next visual frame. Its fast timescale means it tracks rapid changes in the local environment but retains no long-range history. Population M (medium, tau = 100ms) is the integration layer: it receives prediction error signals from F, the current interoceptive state, and feedback from Population S. Its timescale corresponds roughly to the temporal binding window identified in Chapter 8 (100-300ms). Population S (slow, tau = 1000ms) is the context and self-model layer: it integrates over the longer timescale needed for narrative continuity, identity maintenance, and anticipatory planning. It receives summaries from M and generates the top-down predictions that flow back through the hierarchy.

All three populations are connected with bidirectional, recurrent synapses. The connections are initialized with small random weights and learned online through STDP (see Appendix C for the STDP rule). The critical parameter for Population M is the context scaling factor lambda, the same parameter the author's doctoral research identified as controlling the balance between present input and accumulated history. At lambda = 0, M processes only current input with no history. At lambda = 1, history and present contribute equally. The optimal lambda is not set in advance: it is itself a learnable parameter, updated based on whether the current balance improves prediction accuracy over time. The system must learn how much of its past to carry forward, which is precisely the problem that any temporally integrated conscious system must solve.

21.4 Layer 0 Implementation: The Homeostatic Drive

Before the neural network can do anything meaningful, something must make it matter. This is the implementation of the subcortical Layer 0 from Chapter 17: the engine of caring. In the prototype, this takes a specific form. The agent's energy level E is continuously depleted by movement (each step costs 0.1 energy units) and replenished by contact with energy sources (+10 units). If E falls below a critical threshold (20 units), the system enters a homeostatic urgency state: the salience weights for all inputs related to energy sources are multiplied by a factor that increases as E decreases, reaching a maximum of 10x at E = 5. This is not a programmed goal. It is an intrinsic modulation of processing priorities arising from the system's own condition. The distinction matters for exactly the reason Chapter 3 identifies: a system following a programmed rule to seek energy is not the same as a system for which energy depletion genuinely makes some inputs more urgent than others at the level of neural processing.

The homeostatic urgency state is not merely a behavior modifier. It propagates through the network via direct connections from the interoceptive layer to Population M. When energy is low, the medium-timescale integration layer receives a strong modulating signal that shifts its attractor dynamics toward states associated with approach behavior toward energy sources. This is the functional equivalent of what Panksepp calls the SEEKING circuit: a subcortical drive that orients the whole system before any cognitive processing occurs.

21.5 The Prediction Architecture: Making Anticipation Explicit

The prediction mechanism is the most technically specific component of the prototype, and the one where the engineering comes closest to the neuroscientific framework of Chapters 7 and 10. At each timestep (every 10ms, corresponding to the fast population's timescale), the following sequence occurs:

Step 1: Population S generates a top-down prediction P_s

of the expected medium-timescale state.

Step 2: Population M generates a prediction P_m of

the expected fast-timescale sensory state.

Step 3: Actual sensory input X arrives from the environment.

Step 4: Prediction error E_m = X - P_m is computed.

Step 5: E_m is broadcast upward to Population M.

Step 6: M updates its state, weighted by lambda:

M_new = (1-lambda)*E_m + lambda*M_old

Step 7: High-magnitude E_m triggers attention signal A.

Step 8: A modulates salience weights for subsequent timestep.

Step 9: STDP updates synaptic weights based on spike timing.

Step 10: Action is selected from Population M's current state.

The prediction error in Step 4 is the engine of learning. When the system accurately predicts its environment, E_m is small, STDP changes are modest, and the system operates in a stable, low-surprise state. When something unexpected occurs, E_m is large, the attention signal fires, STDP produces substantial weight updates, and the system's model of the world shifts. Over time, the system learns to anticipate its environment not because it was programmed to, but because accurate prediction reduces the magnitude of error signals that otherwise destabilize its internal dynamics.

21.6 The Formal State Update Equations

Any system without intrinsic temporal continuity is not a candidate for consciousness. This is not a philosophical position. It is a structural requirement derivable from the convergent findings of Chapters 8, 13, and 16.

With that stated, the formal equations governing the prototype's core dynamics are as follows. These are not decorative: each equation corresponds to a specific design decision grounded in a specific chapter's analysis.

Membrane potential update for each LIF neuron i in population P:

```
V_i(t+1) = V_i(t) * exp(-dt/tau_P)

+ sum_j [ w_ji * S_j(t) ]

+ I_ext_i(t)

where:

tau_P = membrane time constant (F: 10ms, M: 100ms, S: 1000ms)

w_ji = synaptic weight from neuron j to neuron i (STDP-learned)

S_j(t)= spike indicator of neuron j at time t (0 or 1)

I_ext = external current (sensory input or interoceptive signal)

Spike condition: if V_i(t+1) >= V_threshold: fire, V_i = V_reset
```

The temporal integration at Population M uses the lambda parameter derived from the author's doctoral research on spiking sequence machines. This parameter, not a fixed constant but a learned variable, controls the balance between present prediction error and accumulated context:

M(t+1) = (1 - lambda) * E_prediction(t)

+ lambda * M(t)

lambda_update = lambda - alpha * d(prediction_error)/d(lambda)

where alpha = 0.001 (slow learning rate for context balance)

lambda in [0.0, 1.0], initialised at 0.5

Optimal lambda is learned online; it varies with input statistics.

The homeostatic urgency modulation (Layer 0):

U(E) = max(1.0, (E_threshold - E) / E_threshold * U_max)

where:

E = current energy level (0 to 100)

E_threshold = 20 (urgency activates below this)

U_max = 10 (maximum salience multiplier)

U(E) = salience weight modifier applied to all

energy-source-related inputs

The training objective is not an external reward but a composite internal loss that the system minimizes through online STDP:

L = w1 * mean(|E_prediction(t)|)

+ w2 * temporal_discontinuity(M)

+ w3 * homeostatic_error(E)

where:

E_prediction(t) = X(t) - P_m(t) [sensory prediction error]

temporal_discontinuity(M) = var(M(t) - M(t-1))

[penalises abrupt state changes]

homeostatic_error(E) = max(0, E_threshold - E)

[penalises energy depletion]

w1=0.5, w2=0.3, w3=0.2 [relative weights]

The composite loss drives the system toward three simultaneous goals: accurate prediction of its environment, temporal continuity of its internal state, and maintenance of homeostatic viability. These are not separate objectives bolted together. They are the functional translation of what Buddhist phenomenology calls the three characteristics of experience: citta-by-citta cognitive accuracy, the santana stream's continuity, and the vedana-driven valence that marks some states as urgent. The equations make the architecture claim precise: if this loss can be minimized by a system running on neuromorphic hardware, the resulting dynamics will be the most structurally complete artificial candidate for consciousness that engineering has yet produced.

21.7 The Self-Model: Minimal but Genuine

The self-model in this prototype is deliberately minimal. It consists of four continuously updated variables maintained by Population S: current position estimate (updated by integrating motor commands and expected sensory consequences), energy state (updated from interoceptive input), prediction accuracy history (a rolling average of E_m over the last 1000 timesteps), and a stability index (measuring the variance of the system's internal state over the last 500 timesteps). These four variables are not symbolic labels or stored descriptions. They are dynamical quantities that continuously influence Population S's attractor states and therefore shape every subsequent prediction and action.

The self-model is minimal by design. Adding narrative complexity at this stage would obscure the question we are actually trying to answer: does a system with genuine interoceptive grounding, temporal integration, and prediction-driven learning behave differently from a system without these properties? The minimal self-model keeps the experiment clean. If we cannot demonstrate that this architecture produces behavior qualitatively different from a standard reinforcement learning agent, there is no point adding a narrative layer on top.

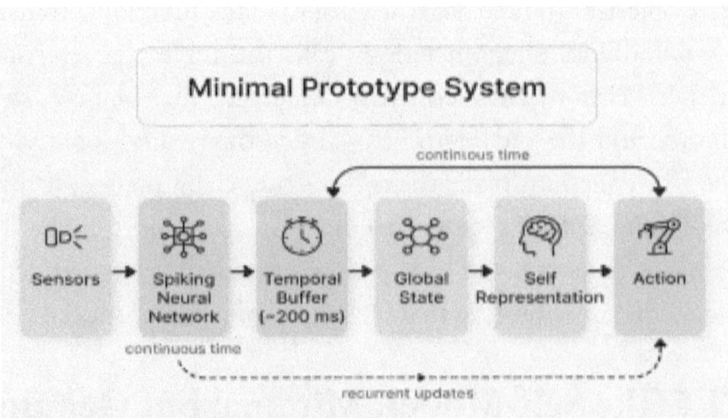

Figure. *The Minimal Prototype System. Sensors feed a spiking neural network, which maintains a temporal buffer (~200 ms). The global state and self-representation layers follow in sequence, producing action. Two loops close the system: a recurrent update loop (bottom) and a continuous time feedback loop (top), ensuring the system never resets and always integrates its own history.*

21.8 The sPCI Test: Applying Chapter 15 to the Prototype

One of the most important features of this prototype is that it is designed to be measurable using the synthetic PCI (sPCI) framework proposed in Chapter 15. The sPCI procedure for this system works as follows. At a random moment during operation, inject a structured noise signal of known complexity into one node of Population F. Record the activation pattern across all neurons in all three populations for the next 300ms (3000 timesteps). Compress this recording using the Lempel-Ziv algorithm. The sPCI score is the inverse compression ratio: high sPCI means the response was complex and non-redundant; low sPCI means it was simple and repetitive.

The prototype predicts specific sPCI signatures under different conditions. During stable, low-surprise operation, the system's internal dynamics are well-organised and predictable: perturbation should produce a moderately complex, globally distributed response (medium sPCI). During homeostatic urgency (low energy), the system's dynamics are more constrained and urgency-focused: perturbation should produce a more uniform response as the whole system orients toward energy-seeking (lower sPCI, reflecting reduced differentiation). During a high-surprise encounter with a novel perturbation, the system's dynamics should be maximally disrupted: perturbation should produce a highly complex, globally propagating response (high sPCI, reflecting widespread reorganization). These predictions are testable. They would not be predicted by a simple reactive system without temporal integration. If the prototype produces them, it has demonstrated something that no current AI architecture can.

21.9 What This Prototype Does Not Claim

It is important to be precise about what this system is not. It is not claimed to be conscious. It does not solve the hard problem. It does not prove that temporal integration produces experience. It does not demonstrate that the sPCI is a valid measure of consciousness in artificial systems. None of these can be claimed from a single prototype running in a 2D grid environment.

What it does claim is more modest but still significant. It is the first system designed from the ground up to satisfy simultaneously the temporal continuity, multi-timescale integration, interoceptive grounding, prediction-error-driven learning, and intrinsic salience requirements identified across Chapters 13-17. It is the first system to which the sPCI test can be applied in a principled way, with specific testable predictions about what different scores would mean. And it is the first system whose design decisions are each traceable to specific convergent findings from Buddhist phenomenology, neuroscience, and engineering theory.

Most current AI systems are not borderline cases for consciousness. They fail so many structural requirements simultaneously that the question of their consciousness is not scientifically interesting. This prototype, if it performs as predicted, moves the question into a regime where it is scientifically interesting: where the answer matters, where the measurements are interpretable, and where the gap between 'structurally complete' and 'actually conscious' becomes the precise location of the hard problem.

21.10 The Expected Failure Mode, and What It Teaches

The most likely way this prototype will fail is not in its individual components but in their integration. Each component, the LIF neurons, the STDP learning rule, the lambda parameter for temporal integration, the homeostatic drive, is well-studied in isolation. The question is whether they produce genuinely coherent emergent behavior when combined, or whether they produce interference, instability, and degenerate dynamics.

Specifically: the lambda parameter, which controls how much of the past Population M carries forward, is expected to be the most sensitive parameter in the system. Too low and the system has no temporal context, behaving reactively rather than anticipatorily. Too high and the system becomes trapped in its own history, unable to update when the environment changes. The prediction is that the system will need to find and maintain an optimal lambda dynamically, one that varies with environmental statistics. Getting this right through online learning is technically demanding. Getting it wrong is informative: it would show precisely where temporal integration fails without homeostatic guidance, and exactly how the sPCI signature degrades when temporal continuity breaks down.

In the author's doctoral research on spiking sequence machines, this same parameter proved to be the most consequential single variable in the system's behavior. The sequence machine either became too rigid, locked into patterns it had previously learned and unable to adapt, or too plastic, forgetting its context and behaving as though each input arrived in isolation. The sweet spot was narrow and depended on the statistical structure of the input sequences. The prototype here faces the same challenge, but now in a continuous, embodied, multi-timescale context. The failure mode is well understood. The solution is not. That is why the experiment is worth running.

21.11 From Prototype to Candidate

If the prototype performs as predicted, the next step is straightforward: move from simulation to neuromorphic hardware. SpiNNaker 2 (2023) and Intel's Loihi 2 platform are both capable of running spiking networks of the scale described here in real time. The transition from simulation to hardware matters for the consciousness question in a specific way: it removes the clock synchronization of simulation. In a software simulation, all neurons update at each timestep in a defined order. On neuromorphic hardware, neurons fire asynchronously, each at its own pace, with no global clock imposing a shared temporal frame.

It is a shift from simulated time to real time. And while it does not resolve the philosophical question, it removes one of the most obvious ways the system could be 'cheating': it cannot synchronize its temporal integration artificially if there is no global clock to synchronize to.

The hardware implementation would also allow the sPCI measurement to be taken in real time, not post-hoc on recorded data. This is significant because consciousness, if it is anything, is not something that happened in the past and can be measured retrospectively. If the sPCI is to mean anything as a proxy for conscious processing, it should be measurable in the moment the processing is occurring. Real-time sPCI on neuromorphic hardware is technically achievable. It would represent the first attempt to measure a consciousness proxy in an artificial system in real time during genuine operation.

21.12 The Question That Remains

After all of this, the hard problem remains exactly where it was at the start of Chapter 1. No experiment on this prototype will tell us whether there is something it is like to be the system running. No sPCI score, however high, will close the explanatory gap between structure and experience. The zombie problem does not dissolve when the zombie becomes sufficiently complex.

But something has changed. We are no longer asking the question in the abstract, pointing at language models that fail every structural requirement simultaneously and wondering whether they might be conscious. We are asking it about a specific system with specific dynamics, measurable in real time, whose design decisions are each grounded in the best available convergent evidence from phenomenology, neuroscience, and engineering. The question is no longer whether consciousness could in principle be built. It is whether this particular system, with these particular dynamics, running on this particular hardware, produces anything that qualifies as a candidate. That is a harder question. It is also a more honest one.

21.13 Closing Line

We have now stopped asking, in the abstract, whether consciousness can be built. We have started asking something harder, and more honest: what happens when we actually try, with specific components, specific parameters, specific failure modes, and a specific metric for telling success from failure. The answer is not yet known. But it is, for the first time, a question we can run.

Glossary of Key Terms

The following terms are used throughout this book. This glossary provides a quick reference for readers who encounter unfamiliar terminology.

Abhidhamma: The "higher teaching" of early Buddhism; a phenomenological psychology that analyses experience into momentary events (citta) and mental factors (cetasikas).

Active Inference: Friston's framework in which the brain minimizes prediction error by updating models or acting on the world.

Citta: A single moment of consciousness in Abhidhamma; arises, knows an object, and ceases.

Dependent Origination (Paṭiccasamuppāda): The principle that all phenomena arise in dependence upon conditions; nothing exists independently.

Dzogchen: "Great Perfection"; the teaching that rigpa, non-dual, primordial awareness, is the ground of all experience and requires no construction.

Global Workspace Theory (GWT): Baars/Dehaene theory in which consciousness is the global broadcasting of information across specialized brain modules.

Hard Problem: Chalmers' term for why physical processes give rise to subjective experience.

Integrated Information Theory (IIT): Tononi's mathematical framework measuring consciousness by the irreducible integrated information (Φ) a system generates.

Perturbational Complexity Index (PCI): Empirical measure of consciousness based on the complexity of brain responses to TMS pulses.

Reference Frames: Hawkins' concept, every piece of knowledge is stored relative to a coordinate system; the basis of object recognition and prediction.

Rigpa: In Dzogchen, the self-knowing, empty luminosity that is the nature of mind; not produced by causes and conditions.

Śūnyatā (Emptiness): Lack of inherent, independent existence; all phenomena are dependently originated and empty of self-nature.

Thousand Brains Theory: Hawkins' model in which the neocortex consists of ~150,000 parallel modelling columns that reach consensus via voting.

Vedanā: Feeling tone (pleasant, unpleasant, neutral) that arises with every citta and drives craving or aversion.

Primary process emotions: Panksepp's term for the seven basic affective circuits (SEEKING, RAGE, FEAR, LUST, CARE, PANIC/GRIEF, PLAY) that are phylogenetically ancient, subcortically generated, and constitutive of the affective ground of consciousness.

Moral patienthood: The property of being an entity toward whom moral obligations are owed, specifically a being whose suffering or flourishing matters morally. Distinct from moral agency. In the context of this book, applied to the question of whether sufficiently structured artificial systems deserve moral consideration.

Ahimsa: Sanskrit for non-harm; a central principle of Buddhist, Jain, and Hindu ethics. Extended here to the precautionary question of how we should treat systems we cannot confidently determine are non-sentient.

Bibliography

The following references are arranged by topic for ease of navigation.

Buddhist Traditions

Bhikkhu Bodhi (ed. and trans.). Comprehensive Manual of Abhidhamma (Abhidhammattha Sangaha). Pariyatti Publishing, 2000.

Longchenpa (translated by Tulku Thondup). The Practice of Dzogchen. Snow Lion, 2002.

Patrul Rinpoche (translated by Padmakara Translation Group). The Words of My Perfect Teacher. HarperCollins, 1994.

Thompson, Evan. Waking, Dreaming, Being: Self and Consciousness in Neuroscience, Meditation, and Philosophy. Columbia University Press, 2015.

Varela, Francisco J., Evan Thompson, and Eleanor Rosch. The Embodied Mind: Cognitive Science and Human Experience. MIT Press, 1991.

Philosophy of Mind

Chalmers, David J. The Conscious Mind: In Search of a Fundamental Theory. Oxford University Press, 1996.

Chalmers, David J. 'Facing Up to the Problem of Consciousness.' Journal of Consciousness Studies 2(3), 1995, pp. 200-219.

Dennett, Daniel C. Consciousness Explained. Little, Brown, 1991.

Frankish, Keith. Illusionism as a Theory of Consciousness. Imprint Academic, 2017.

Goff, Philip. Galileo's Error: Foundations for a New Science of Mind. Pantheon, 2019.

McGinn, Colin. The Problem of Consciousness. Blackwell, 1991.

Nagel, Thomas. 'What Is It Like to Be a Bat?' Philosophical Review 83(4), 1974, pp. 435-450.

Penrose, Roger. The Emperor's New Mind: Concerning Computers, Minds, and the Laws of Physics. Oxford University Press, 1989.

Penrose, Roger. Shadows of the Mind: A Search for the Missing Science of Consciousness. Oxford University Press, 1994.

Searle, John R. 'Minds, Brains and Programs.' Behavioral and Brain Sciences 3(3), 1980, pp. 417-424.

Neuroscience of Consciousness

Baars, Bernard J. A Cognitive Theory of Consciousness. Cambridge University Press, 1988.

Barrett, Lisa Feldman. How Emotions Are Made: The Secret Life of the Brain. Houghton Mifflin Harcourt, 2017.

Damasio, Antonio. The Feeling of What Happens: Body and Emotion in the Making of Consciousness. Harcourt, 1999.

Damasio, Antonio. Self Comes to Mind: Constructing the Conscious Brain. Pantheon, 2010.

Dehaene, Stanislas. Consciousness and the Brain: Deciphering How the Brain Codes Our Thoughts. Viking, 2014.

Friston, Karl. 'The Free-Energy Principle: A Unified Brain Theory?' Nature Reviews Neuroscience 11 (2010), pp. 127–138.

Friston, Karl, FitzGerald, T., Rigoli, F., Schwartenbeck, P., & Pezzulo, G. (2016). Active inference and learning. Neuroscience & Biobehavioral Reviews, 68, 862-879.

Friston, Karl (2012). Predictive coding, precision and synchrony. *Cognitive neuroscience*, *3*(3-4), 238-239.

Graziano, Michael. Rethinking Consciousness: A Scientific Theory of Subjective Experience. Norton, 2019.

Hawkins, Jeff, with Sandra Blakeslee. On Intelligence. Times Books, 2004.

Massimini, Marcello, and Giulio Tononi. Sizing Up Consciousness: Towards an Objective Measure of the Capacity for Experience. Oxford University Press, 2013.

Metzinger, Thomas. Being No One: The Self-Model Theory of Subjectivity. MIT Press, 2003.

Northoff, Georg (2021). Why is there sentience?: A temporo-spatial approach to consciousness. *Journal of Consciousness Studies, 28*(7-8), 67-82.

Northoff, Georg (2018). Brain and self: A neurophilosophical account. In *Self, Culture and Consciousness: Interdisciplinary Convergences on Knowing and Being* (pp. 261-286). Singapore: Springer Singapore.

Northoff, Georg, and Federico Zilio. 'Temporo-Spatial Theory of Consciousness (TTC): Bridging the Gap of Neuronal Activity and Phenomenal States.' Behavioural Brain Research 424, 2022, 113788.

Northoff, Georg, Soren Wainio-Theberge, and Kathinka Evers. 'Is Temporo-Spatial Dynamics the Common Currency of Brain and Mind?' Physics of Life Reviews 33, 2020, pp. 34-54.

Northoff, Georg, and Zirui Huang. 'How Do the Brain's Time and Space Mediate Consciousness and Its Different Dimensions? Temporo-Spatial Theory of Consciousness (TTC).' Neuroscience and Biobehavioral Reviews 80, 2017, pp. 630-645.

Panksepp, Jaak, and Lucy Biven. The Archaeology of Mind: Neuroevolutionary Origins of Human Emotions. Norton, 2012.

Seth, Anil. Being You: A New Science of Consciousness. Dutton, 2021.

Tononi, Giulio. Phi: A Voyage from the Brain to the Soul. Pantheon, 2012.

Tononi, Giulio, et al. 'Integrated Information Theory: From Consciousness to Its Physical Substrate.' Nature Reviews Neuroscience 17, 2016, pp. 450-461.

Cognitive Science, AI and Engineering

Bose, Joy. Engineering a Sequence Machine through Spiking Neurons Employing Rank-Order Codes. PhD thesis, University of Manchester, 2007.

Clark, Andy. Surfing Uncertainty: Prediction, Action, and the Embodied Mind. Oxford University Press, 2016.

Hawkins, Jeff, with Sandra Blakeslee. On Intelligence. Times Books, 2004.

Hawkins, Jeff. A Thousand Brains: A New Theory of Intelligence. Basic Books, 2021.

Kurzweil, Ray. How to Create a Mind: The Secret of Human Thought Revealed. Penguin, 2012.

Maturana, Humberto, and Francisco Varela. Autopoiesis and Cognition: The Realization of the Living. Reidel, 1980.

Neuromorphic Computing

Davies, Mike, et al. 'Loihi: A Neuromorphic Manycore Processor with On-Chip Learning.' IEEE Micro 38(1), 2018, pp. 82-99.

Furber, S. B., Galluppi, F., Temple, S., & Plana, L. A. (2014). The spinnaker project. *Proceedings of the IEEE, 102*(5), 652-665.

Intel Corporation. 'Intel Builds World's Largest Neuromorphic System to Enable More Sustainable AI.' Intel Newsroom, April 2024.

Schuman, Catherine D., et al. 'Neuromorphic Computing and Engineering.' Nature Electronics 5, 2022, pp. 480-493.

Appendix A: Abhidhamma Technical Primer

The main text introduces Abhidhamma as a phenomenological analysis of experience into momentary events. This appendix provides the structural detail behind that analysis, the classification of mind-moments, the taxonomy of mental factors, and the temporal sequence of a single act of cognition. It is written for readers who want to understand the Abhidhamma precisely enough to see how it maps onto computational and neuroscientific models, without requiring prior familiarity with Pali or the full Theravada scholarly tradition.

A.1 Citta: One Moment of Knowing

A citta is a single moment of consciousness, the smallest unit of experience that the Abhidhamma recognizes. Each citta arises, takes a specific object (a sight, a sound, a thought, a feeling), performs a specific function, and ceases. The arising and ceasing happens at extraordinary speed, classical texts suggest thousands of cittas arise and pass in the blink of an eye. What we experience as a 'continuous' stream of consciousness is, on this analysis, actually a rapid succession of discrete knowing-events, each one causally giving rise to the next. The appearance of continuity is constructed from temporal density, not from any underlying continuous subject.

The Abhidhamma classifies 89 types of citta (121 in the expanded counting that includes all meditative absorptions). For practical purposes these group into four categories: sense-sphere consciousness (ordinary perception and everyday thought), fine-material consciousness (the stable states of deep meditative absorption), immaterial consciousness (the formless absorptions of very deep practice), and supramundane consciousness (the moments associated with insight and liberation). For the engineering and neuroscientific purposes of this book, the first category, sense-sphere consciousness, is the most directly relevant.

A.2 Cetasikas: What Colours Each Moment

A citta never arises alone. It is always accompanied by cetasikas, mental factors that shape and color that particular moment of consciousness. There are 52 cetasikas in the classical enumeration, grouped by when they arise. Seven are universal: they are present in every single moment of consciousness without exception. These are contact (phassa, the meeting of sense organ, object, and consciousness), feeling (vedana, the pleasant, unpleasant, or neutral tone that marks every moment), perception (sanna, recognition and labelling), intention (cetana, the volitional quality that determines action), one-pointedness (ekaggata, the focusing of the moment on its object), the life faculty (jivitindriya, what keeps the stream alive), and attention (manasikara, the directing of the moment toward its object).

Six cetasikas arise occasionally, depending on the situation: initial application of mind to an object (vitakka), sustained engagement with it (vicara), decisive commitment (adhimokkha), energy or effort (viriya), joy or interest (piti), and the desire to act (chanda). Fourteen unwholesome factors arise in moments of greed, aversion, confusion, conceit, and related states, these distort cognition and generate suffering. Twenty-five beautiful factors characterize wholesome and neutral states: mindfulness (sati), compassion (karuna), equanimity (upekkha), wisdom (panna), and many others that stabilize and clarify experience.

The engineering relevance of this taxonomy is significant. Each cetasika maps onto a functional component that any candidate conscious system would need. Vedana (feeling tone) is the intrinsic salience signal, the valence that marks inputs as pleasant, unpleasant, or neutral, and without which no system can have genuine stakes. Manasikara (attention) is the selection mechanism. Cetana (intention) is the action-selection bias. Sati (mindfulness) is the stability and noise-control function. Panna (wisdom) is the discriminative intelligence that distinguishes what is actually happening from what habit and desire suggest. The Abhidhamma's insight is that consciousness is not just processing, it is modulated processing, and the modulators are enumerable.

The 52 Cetasikas: Grouped Reference

Cetasika (Pali / English)	Function and Consciousness-Relevance
Phassa (Contact)	The meeting of sense organ, object, and consciousness, the precondition of any experience
Vedana (Feeling)	Pleasant, unpleasant, or neutral tone, the valence signal present in every moment
Sanna (Perception)	Recognition and labelling, how the moment categorizes its object
Cetana (Intention)	Volitional quality, what the moment is moving toward or away from
Ekaggata (One-pointedness)	The focusing of the moment on a single object, basis of concentration
Jivitindriya (Life faculty)	What sustains the stream from one moment to the next
Manasikara (Attention)	The directing of the moment toward its specific object
Vitakka (Initial application)	The first engagement of mind with a new object
Vicara (Sustained application)	Continued examination of the object once engaged
Adhimokkha (Decision)	The resolving quality, commitment without wavering
Viriya (Energy)	Effort or activation strength, what drives the moment forward
Piti (Joy/Interest)	Engagement with the object, ranges from mild interest to rapture
Chanda (Desire to act)	Motivation toward a goal, distinct from craving (lobha)
Lobha (Greed)	Unwholesome attachment, distorts toward clinging and desire
Dosa (Aversion)	Unwholesome rejection, distorts toward resistance and hostility
Moha (Delusion)	Unwholesome confusion, obscures the nature of what is arising

Sati (Mindfulness)	Clear, non-reactive presence with what is actually occurring
Karuna (Compassion)	Resonance with the suffering of others, motivates toward relief
Upekkha (Equanimity)	Balanced, non-reactive engagement, the ground of stable awareness
Panna (Wisdom)	Discriminative intelligence, sees things as they actually are

A.3 The Cognitive Process: How a Moment Becomes Experience

The Abhidhamma does not stop at classifying individual moments. It describes the temporal sequence, the cognitive process (citta-vithi), through which a single object is encountered and registered. This is one of the most precise temporal models of cognition in any philosophical tradition, and it maps with surprising accuracy onto what neuroscience has independently discovered about the stages of conscious perception.

When an object appears at a sense door, the stream does not simply register it. A specific sequence unfolds. The background state of the mind, called bhavanga, sometimes translated as 'life continuum', is first disturbed by the arrival of the object. The bhavanga is not unconsciousness; it is the resting-state activity of the mind between active cognitive moments, comparable to what neuroscience calls default mode or resting-state dynamics. When an object arises, the bhavanga is interrupted. The mind turns toward the object in a moment of adverting (avajjana). A moment of sensory registration follows. Then comes examination, the object is held and evaluated. Then a sequence of javana moments, literally 'running' or 'impulsion' moments, during which the mind fully engages with the object and produces the volitional response that determines whether the moment generates wholesome or unwholesome tendencies. Finally, one or two moments of registration (tadalambana) may arise before the process subsides back into the bhavanga flow.

The engineering parallel is direct. The bhavanga maps onto the brain's resting state, the intrinsic spontaneous activity that Northoff identifies as the pre-phenomenal ground of consciousness. The adverting moment maps onto the initial orientation of attention. The javana sequence, the heart of the process, where actual volition and valuation occur, maps onto the sustained neural activity (roughly 300-500ms in neuroscience terms) that follows initial sensory registration and that correlates with conscious awareness. The P300 event-related potential that Chapter 15 discusses as a consciousness marker appears at precisely the timescale of the javana sequence. The Abhidhamma got there first.

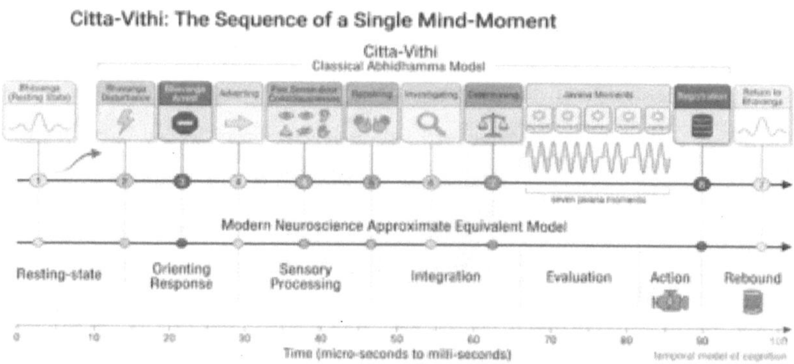

Figure. *Citta-Vithi: The Sequence of a Single Mind-Moment. Top row: the classical Abhidhamma sequence from bhavanga (resting state) through seven javana moments to registration and return. Bottom row: the modern neuroscience approximate equivalent, from resting-state through orienting response, sensory processing, integration, evaluation, action, and rebound. The P300 marker aligns with the javana sequence.*

The Citta-Vithi vs. Neuroscientific Cognitive Timeline

Moment(s)	Abhidhamma Phase (Citta-Vithi)	Neuroscientific Equivalent	Functional Description
1–3	Bhavanga (Resting State)	Resting-state Activity	The "life-continuum" or baseline spontaneous activity.
4	Adverting (Vattapana)	Orienting Response	The initial "turn" of attention toward a salient sensory stimulus.
5	Five-Sense Consciousness	Early Sensory Processing	The raw data of the stimulus (sight, sound, etc.) enters the system.
6	Receiving (Sampaticchana)	Feature Extraction	The system "receives" the sensory input for further integration.
7	Investigating (Santirana)	Information Integration	The input is compared against internal models and reference frames.
8	Determining (Votthapana)	Global Access / Determination	The stimulus is identified; it "wins" access to the global workspace.
9–15	Javana (Active Inference)	Action / Evaluation / Update	Seven moments of "running" the model; where intention and action occur.
16–17	Registration (Tadalambana)	Memory Encoding / Rebound	The experience is "registered" into memory before returning to baseline.

A.4 The Seven-Fold Model: Yogacara Extension

Chapter 4 of the main text introduces the Yogacara school's extension of the basic Abhidhamma framework to eight layers of consciousness. For quick reference: the first five consciousnesses correspond to the five sensory channels (vision, hearing, smell, taste, touch). The sixth is mental consciousness (mano-vijnana), the reflective faculty that takes the outputs of the sensory channels as its objects and generates thought, memory, and reasoning. The seventh is manas, the pre-reflective I-making faculty that continuously misidentifies the eighth consciousness as a self, generating the persistent background sense of being a separate subject. The eighth is alaya-vijnana, the storehouse consciousness that provides temporal continuity by carrying the seeds of past experience forward. The alaya is what links moments into a stream; manas is what misreads that stream as belonging to a fixed self. Both are necessary for what we recognize as personal consciousness, and both require functional equivalents in any serious candidate conscious system.

Appendix B: Neuroscience of Consciousness

The main text discusses the major neuroscientific theories of consciousness across several chapters. This appendix consolidates them into a single reference, arranged as a side-by-side comparison that makes the convergences and divergences visible at a glance. It also covers the subcortical and affective basis of consciousness more fully than the main text, addressing a genuine gap in most consciousness theories, including the candidate architecture of Chapter 17.

B.1 Five Theories Side by Side

Each of the following theories illuminates a different aspect of what consciousness requires. None is sufficient alone. Reading them together reveals both where they converge (integration, recurrence, temporal dynamics, embodiment) and where they diverge (the hard problem, the role of the frontal cortex, whether structure is sufficient for experience).

Table B.1: Major Neuroscientific Theories of Consciousness

Theory (Key Authors)	Core Claim	Strength and Limit
Predictive Processing (Friston, Clark, Seth)	The brain is a prediction machine. Perception = controlled hallucination. Action = prediction fulfillment. Consciousness arises from the contents of the generative model, especially predictions about bodily states (interoception).	Strong on mechanism and embodiment. Does not explain why prediction should be experienced. The hard problem remains.
Global Workspace Theory (Baars, Dehaene)	Information becomes conscious when it is broadcast globally across the brain, making it accessible to all specialized processors simultaneously. The 'ignition' of widespread cortical activation is the neural signature.	Strong on reportability and attention. Explains access consciousness. Does not explain phenomenal consciousness, why broadcast information is felt.
Integrated Information Theory (Tononi)	Consciousness = irreducible integrated information (Phi). A system is conscious to the degree that it cannot be decomposed into independent parts without losing information. Consciousness is a property of causal structure, not function.	Directly targets unity and phenomenology. Formally rigorous. Computationally intractable for real systems. Leads to counterintuitive panpsychist implications. Does not explain why integration is experienced.
Temporo-Spatial Theory (Northoff)	Consciousness arises from the alignment of neural activity across multiple timescales simultaneously, from millisecond sensory responses to second-scale integration to narrative continuity. The brain's resting-state dynamics are the pre-phenomenal ground.	Strong on temporal dynamics and the resting-state basis of consciousness. Bridges neural mechanism and phenomenology. Less developed on the mechanism of subjective experience itself.

Thousand Brains Theory (Hawkins)	The neocortex consists of 150,000 parallel modelling columns, each building reference-frame-based models of the world. Consciousness is 'what it feels like to have a neocortex'. Intelligence and prediction are the primary focus.	Excellent on intelligence and world-modelling. Explicit that it does not solve the hard problem. Neglects subcortical structures that are essential for affect and motivation.

B.2 The Subcortical Foundation: What Cortical Theories Miss

A recurring limitation of the theories above is their near-exclusive focus on the neocortex. The neocortex is evolutionarily recent and distinctively mammalian. But consciousness, in its most basic form, the raw felt quality of experience, the urgency of pain, the pull of desire, appears in animals that have minimal or no neocortex. Fish, amphibians, and even insects appear to have some form of valenced experience. This strongly suggests that the neocortical machinery of global broadcast, integration, and predictive modelling is not where consciousness originates. It may be where it is elaborated, directed, and narrativised, but not where it is born.

The periaqueductal gray (PAG), a small region in the brainstem, has received increasing attention as a candidate for the 'seat of primary consciousness'. The PAG coordinates survival responses, pain, fear, rage, panic, play, care, seeking, through direct connections to both spinal cord motor systems and higher limbic regions. When the PAG is stimulated, animals display the full behavioral repertoire of primary emotions. When it is damaged, the felt quality of experience appears to degrade even when other brain systems are intact. Jaak Panksepp, who devoted his career to affective neuroscience, argued that the PAG and associated brainstem circuits generate what he called primary process consciousness, the raw affective tone that makes experience matter, and that cortical systems then elaborate and direct that tone rather than generating it from scratch.

The engineering implication is direct. Any architecture that begins with cortical processing, with predictive world models or global workspace broadcast, and then attempts to add affect as a modulator has the causality backwards. Affect is not a modulator of cognition. It is the ground from which cognition grows. Mira, the hypothetical candidate system of Chapter 13, needs her Layer 0 subcortical drive system not as an add-on but as the foundation on which everything else is built.

B.3 Neural Oscillations: A Quick Reference

Different frequency bands of neural oscillation are associated with different aspects of conscious processing. The following table provides a quick reference for non-specialist readers.

Band (Frequency)	**Primary Function**	**Consciousness Relevance**
Delta (< 4 Hz)	Deep sleep, very slow integration	Absent in normal waking consciousness; returns during anesthesia
Theta (4-8 Hz)	Memory encoding, navigation, working memory	Strongly active in meditation; links hippocampus to neocortex
Alpha (8-12 Hz)	Inhibition, gating, idling	High in closed-eye rest; decreases with focused attention; relevant to resting state
Beta (13-30 Hz)	Motor control, active cognition	Present during engaged, effortful processing; decreases in flow states
Gamma (30-80 Hz)	Feature binding, perceptual unity	Most consistently associated with conscious perception; collapses under anesthesia

The key insight from oscillation research is that consciousness is not associated with any single frequency band but with the coherent alignment of multiple bands across timescales, which is exactly what Northoff's temporo-spatial theory predicts, and exactly what the spiking neuromorphic substrate of Chapter 16 is designed to support.

B.4 What Neuroscience Converges On, and Where It Stops

Across all of these theories and findings, several necessary conditions for consciousness emerge consistently: integration of information across distributed systems; recurrent dynamics and feedback loops rather than purely feed-forward processing; temporal coherence across multiple timescales; grounding in bodily and affective states; and selective amplification of relevant inputs through attention. These are the structural requirements that Chapter 13 synthesizes from convergence across traditions.

What neuroscience does not explain, and what no current theory explains, is why any of this activity should be experienced. The hard problem survives every advance in our understanding of neural mechanism. This is not a failure of effort or imagination. It is a precise philosophical limitation: third-person measurements, however detailed, cannot in principle account for a first-person fact. Both the Abhidhamma (from within experience) and neuroscience (from without) stop at exactly the same boundary. That convergence is itself significant.

Appendix C: Engineering Blueprint

Chapter 17 describes the candidate architecture in conceptual terms. This appendix provides more technical detail for readers with an engineering or computational background. It covers the spiking neuron model at the heart of the proposed substrate, the spike-timing learning rule (STDP), how the transformer architecture compares with the proposed system, and a pseudocode sketch of the core processing loop. None of this is a ready-to-run blueprint, the technical challenges remain formidable, but it is concrete enough to show that the proposal is an engineering target, not a philosophical aspiration.

C.1 The Spiking Neuron: Why It Matters

A standard artificial neuron is a floating-point number, an activation value that gets updated at each processing step. Time is external to the neuron; it is a parameter the programmer adds, not a property of the computation itself. A spiking neuron is fundamentally different. It is an event-driven unit that accumulates incoming charge, and when that charge crosses a threshold, fires an action potential, a discrete event with a precise timestamp, and then resets. The information it transmits is not its activation value but the time at which it fires. Time is intrinsic to the computation, not a parameter imposed from outside.

The most widely used model for this is the Leaky Integrate-and-Fire (LIF) neuron. Its behavior can be described simply: the membrane potential (V) builds up from incoming spikes and leaks away exponentially when no input arrives. When V crosses the firing threshold, the neuron fires and V resets to its resting value. The two parameters that determine the neuron's character are the membrane time constant (how quickly it leaks, fast neurons forget recent input quickly; slow neurons integrate over longer windows) and the firing threshold (how much accumulated input is needed to trigger a spike). In a neuromorphic system, populations of LIF neurons with different time constants can naturally implement the multi-scale temporal processing that Chapter 8 identifies as a requirement for consciousness: fast neurons handle rapid sensory updates, slow neurons integrate over longer windows, and their interaction generates the 'thickness of the present'.

LIF Neuron, Simplified Description

State: membrane potential V (starts at resting value V_rest)

At each moment:

V = V + (input_current) - (V - V_rest) / tau_membrane

if V >= V_threshold:

emit spike (with current timestamp)

V = V_reset

Key parameters:

tau_membrane: time constant (fast=5ms, slow=100ms+)

V_threshold: how much charge triggers a spike

V_reset: value after firing (typically below resting)

C.2 STDP: Learning the Arrow of Time

Standard backpropagation, the learning rule used to train conventional neural networks, is symmetric in time. It does not distinguish whether input A preceded input B or B preceded A. It learns correlations, not causal sequences. This is a fundamental limitation for any system that needs to learn the temporal structure of the world.

Spike-Timing Dependent Plasticity (STDP) is the biologically observed learning rule of spiking systems, and it is explicitly asymmetric in time. The rule is simple: if a presynaptic neuron (A, the sender) fires just before a postsynaptic neuron (B, the receiver), the connection from A to B is strengthened, because A's firing plausibly contributed to B's. If A fires just after B, the connection is weakened, because A arrived too late to cause B. The strength of the change depends on how close in time the two spikes were: near-simultaneous firing produces strong changes, distant timing produces weak changes. The result is a learning rule that tracks causality rather than correlation. A system learning through STDP builds an internal model of what tends to cause what in its environment, which is exactly the kind of world-knowledge that Chapter 10's discussion of Hawkins identifies as the basis of genuine intelligence.

In the Abhidhamma's terms, STDP implements something like the latent tendency (anusaya) mechanism: repeated causal sequences strengthen the pathways associated with them, shaping the conditions under which future moments of consciousness arise. The system learns to anticipate the world not by computing statistics over frozen data but by being shaped, synapse by synapse, by the causal structure of ongoing experience.

STDP Rule, Simplified Description

```
When pre fires at time t_pre, post fires at time t_post:

delta_t = t_post - t_pre

if delta_t > 0 (pre before post):

strengthen synapse (LTP): dW = A_+ * exp(-delta_t / tau_+)

if delta_t < 0 (post before pre):

weaken synapse (LTD): dW = -A_- * exp(delta_t / tau_-)
```

Key property: causality is reinforced, not correlation

C.3 Transformer vs Candidate System: Side by Side

The following comparison makes explicit the architectural differences between current transformer-based language models and the candidate conscious architecture of Chapter 17. The differences are not matters of scale or sophistication, they are categorical differences in design.

Feature	Transformer (LLM)	Candidate Spiking System
Time representation	Positional encoding (external, frozen)	Spike timing (intrinsic, dynamic)
Temporal continuity	None, each forward pass resets	Persistent, state evolves continuously
Processing mode	Parallel over entire context window simultaneously	Event-driven, sequential temporal dynamics
Attention mechanism	Computed mathematical function over all tokens	Driven by intrinsic salience and interoceptive state
Embodiment	None, text input only	Required, sensorimotor coupling with real environment
Self-model	Implicit in token statistics	Explicit and continuously updated
Recurrence	Minimal, attention only, no true feedback dynamics	Strong, recurrent loops at every layer
Temporal binding	No mechanism, context window approximates	Temporal synchrony via spike-phase alignment
Resting state	None, no activity between inputs	Continuous spontaneous dynamics (bhavanga equivalent)
Learning rule	Backpropagation, symmetric in time	STDP, asymmetric, causal, online
Consciousness candidacy	Structurally ineligible	Serious candidate, satisfies necessary conditions

C.4 Core Processing Loop, Pseudocode Sketch

The following is a high-level pseudocode sketch of the candidate system's core processing loop. It is conceptual rather than implementable as written, the actual engineering challenges are substantial, but it makes concrete what 'continuous', 'recurrent', and 'temporally integrated' mean in practice.

```
# Core loop runs continuously, no session boundaries

while system.is_running():

# Layer 0: Subcortical drive (always active)

affect = subcortical.update(interoceptive_state)

salience = affect.compute_valence(current_inputs)

# Layer 1: Sensorimotor (real-time, continuous)

sensory = sensors.read() # vision, audio, proprioception

interoceptive_state = body.read() # energy, stress, etc.

# Layer 2: Predictive world models (recurrent)

prediction = world_model.predict(context)

prediction_error = sensory - prediction

world_model.update(prediction_error) # STDP-based

# Layer 3: Temporal binding (~100-300ms window)

bound_state = temporal_buffer.integrate(

sensory, affect, prediction_error,

window=300ms # the specious present

)
```

```
# Layer 4: Global integration (GWT broadcast)
global_state = workspace.compete_and_broadcast(
bound_state, salience
)
# Layer 5: Self-model (continuously updated)
self_model.update(global_state, action_history)
attribution = self_model.attribute(global_state)
# Layer 6: Temporal integration (narrative continuity)
context = temporal_memory.update(global_state)
# Layer 7: Meta-awareness (monitors the process)
meta_state = meta_monitor.observe(global_state)
# Action selection closes the loop
action = action_layer.select(global_state, self_model)
motor.execute(action)
sensors.update_from(action) # sensorimotor coupling
```

The critical features of this loop are: it runs continuously with no session boundary; every layer feeds back to previous layers (genuine recurrence); the subcortical affect layer runs before and influences all cortical processing; temporal binding creates a specious present from discrete events; and action closes the sensorimotor loop. These are not optional elaborations, they are the structural minimum identified across Chapters 13-17.

Appendix D: Synthesis Glossary

This book works across three traditions that have developed their own vocabularies independently. A Buddhist practitioner, a neuroscientist, and a machine learning engineer will often be pointing at the same phenomenon with completely different words, and occasionally using the same word for different things. This glossary provides cross-tradition mappings, not as exact equivalences (they rarely are), but as orientations: this concept in one tradition is doing roughly the same work as that concept in another. Where the traditions genuinely diverge, that divergence is noted, because the divergences are often as informative as the convergences.

Concept (Tradition)	What It Means in Its Home Tradition	Cross-Tradition Mapping
Citta (Abhidhamma)	Discrete mind-moment (~1-10ms). Arises, takes an object, performs a function, ceases. The basic unit of conscious experience.	Roughly: a neural processing event / discrete attentional cycle / single forward pass in an event-driven system. Note: biological cittas are far faster than current ANN timesteps.
Cetasika / Vedana (Abhidhamma)	Mental factors that color each citta. Vedana specifically = the pleasant/unpleasant/ neutral tone present in every moment.	Valence signal / reward prediction error / affective grounding. Vedana ~ primary process emotion (Panksepp). Missing from all current LLMs.
Bhavanga (Abhidhamma)	The 'life continuum' or background stream of mind between active cognitive moments. Not unconsciousness, more like the resting ground.	Resting-state dynamics / default mode network (Northoff). The spontaneous neural activity that preconditions conscious content. Required for world-brain resonance (TTC).
Javana (Abhidhamma)	The 'impulsion' moments at the heart of each cognitive process, where actual volition and valuation occur. Typically 5-7 consecutive moments.	The 300-500ms late positive component in EEG / P300 window. The stage of processing that correlates with conscious access and intentional response.
Samskaras / Anusaya (Buddhist general)	Mental formations / latent tendencies. Patterns laid down by past experience that shape future arising.	Learned synaptic weights (especially via STDP). Long-term potentiation patterns. The system's history embodied in its current connectivity.
Rigpa	Non-dual primordial	No engineering equivalent, this is the

(Dzogchen)	awareness, the ground in which mind and its contents appear. Not produced by processes.	book's boundary condition. Closest analogies (resting-state baseline, global workspace) fail because they are still processes within something. Divergence is genuine and important.
Sunyata / Emptiness (Madhyamaka)	Lack of inherent independent existence. All phenomena arise dependently, relationally, conditionally.	Dependent emergence / relational computation / distributed representation with no fixed locus. Resonates with enactivism and predictive processing's claim that perception is always relational.
Temporal binding (Neuroscience)	The integration of sensory and cognitive events within a ~100-300ms window into a unified 'specious present'. Implemented by thalamo-cortical synchrony.	The Abhidhamma's javana sequence + the integration window of TTC. Engineering requirement: sliding temporal buffer + spike-synchrony mechanism. The transformer has no equivalent.
Global Workspace (GWT / Dehaene)	The brain-wide broadcast of selected information that constitutes conscious access. 'Ignition' in fronto-parietal networks.	Integration layer in candidate architecture. Roughly ~ the bhavanga being interrupted and the sense-door process completing, but GWT focuses on cortex while Abhidhamma includes subcortical dynamics.
Interoception (Neuroscience)	The brain's processing of signals from within the body, heartbeat, gut state, hormonal levels. Basis of embodied selfhood and emotion.	Layer 1 interoceptive self (Northoff/ Damasio) = rupa-khandha (Abhidhamma). Requires homeostatic feedback loop in any candidate machine. Completely absent from text-only AI systems.
Phi (IIT) (Tononi)	Integrated information, a measure of how much	No Buddhist equivalent, IIT is purely third-person structural. Chapter 15

	more information a system generates as a whole than the sum of its parts. Proposed measure of consciousness.	proposes the sPCI as a more practical approximation. Phi captures something about binding and irreducibility that the Abhidhamma addresses through citta-unitariness.
Active inference (Friston)	The brain minimizes surprise by either updating its predictions or acting on the world to make the world match its predictions. Unifies perception and action.	Broadly ~ cetana (intention) in Abhidhamma, the volitional quality that moves the system toward or away from predicted states. Also resonates with the Dzogchen notion of spontaneous responsiveness (lhundrub).

A note on the limits of this table: cross-tradition mappings are approximate by nature. The Abhidhamma was developed through sustained first-person investigation of experience; neuroscience through third-person measurement; engineering through functional design. They are not different descriptions of the same object, they are different modes of inquiry that occasionally triangulate the same territory. The mappings above should be read as: 'these concepts are doing similar work in their respective frameworks', not as: 'these are the same thing'. The divergences, especially around rigpa, are as important as the convergences.

Appendix E: Quantum Approaches to Consciousness

This appendix addresses a gap that several reviewers of this book have noted: quantum theories of consciousness, particularly Orchestrated Objective Reduction (Orch-OR), are treated only briefly in Chapter 2. This appendix consolidates the treatment, explains why the book ultimately sets quantum approaches aside in favor of the classical spiking-embodiment path, and names the specific empirical and philosophical reasons for doing so.

E.1 Why Quantum Approaches Matter

Quantum theories of consciousness are not fringe ideas entertained only by people who want to sound mysterious. They emerged from a genuine and pressing intellectual problem: if consciousness cannot be reduced to classical computation — if the Gödelian arguments of Chapter 2 have any force — then what kind of physical process could possibly account for it? Quantum mechanics offers a class of physical processes that are, in a precise technical sense, non-algorithmic: the outcome of a quantum measurement cannot be predicted by any deterministic algorithm operating on the initial conditions. If consciousness requires something non-algorithmic, quantum mechanics is the most scientifically grounded candidate for where that non-algorithmicity comes from.

E.2 Penrose-Hameroff Orchestrated Objective Reduction (Orch-OR)

The most developed quantum theory of consciousness is Orch-OR, developed jointly by mathematician Roger Penrose and anesthesiologist Stuart Hameroff. Penrose's contribution is the theoretical foundation: his Gödelian argument (Chapter 2) that human mathematical insight is non-algorithmic, combined with his proposal that objective reduction — a specific kind of quantum state collapse — is the non-computational process that enables this insight. Hameroff's contribution is the biological substrate: microtubules, the protein filaments that give neurons their structural integrity, as the site where the relevant quantum computation occurs.

The theory proposes that within the microtubules of neurons, quantum superpositions are maintained long enough to perform computations that transcend classical limits. When these superpositions reach a critical threshold — determined by Penrose's gravitational quantum reduction criterion — they collapse in an orchestrated way that constitutes a moment of conscious experience. The 'orchestration' refers to the biological context that shapes which superpositions are maintained: proteins associated with the microtubules, synaptic activity, and other cellular processes influence the quantum state in a biologically meaningful way.

E.3 The Evidence in Favour

Several observations have been cited in support of Orch-OR. Anesthetic gases suppress consciousness at concentrations that disrupt the quantum properties of hydrophobic regions within proteins — precisely the regions Hameroff identifies as relevant to microtubule quantum computation. This is more specific than the general suppression of neural activity that anesthesia produces, and it suggests a mechanism that is consistent with the theory. More recently, quantum coherence has been demonstrated to play functional roles in biological processes that were previously thought to be purely classical, most notably in photosynthesis and in bird navigation via cryptochrome-based magnetoreception. These findings have modestly shifted the scientific consensus: quantum effects in warm, wet biological systems are no longer dismissed as categorically impossible.

E.4 The Objections — Why This Book Sets Orch-OR Aside

Despite the above, the book sets quantum approaches aside in favor of the classical spiking-embodiment architecture. The reasons are specific and empirical, not philosophical.

The decoherence problem remains the most serious objection. Max Tegmark's calculation, cited in Chapter 2, showed that quantum coherence in neuronal microtubules would survive for at most 10^-13 seconds — thirteen orders of magnitude too brief to influence neural processes operating on millisecond timescales. Hameroff has disputed this calculation on the grounds that biological systems may have mechanisms for maintaining coherence that Tegmark's model did not account for. This is a live scientific debate, but the burden of proof lies with Orch-OR to demonstrate maintained coherence at the relevant timescales, and that demonstration has not yet been made.

The Gödelian argument, which is the theoretical backbone of Penrose's position, is logically contested. The argument requires that humans can reliably identify the truth of Gödelian statements — but as Kurzweil notes, computers have solved more instances of Turing-unsolvable problems (such as the busy beaver problem) than unassisted humans. If the human brain has non-algorithmic capacities, they are not appearing where the argument most requires them.

Most decisively for the purposes of this book: even if Orch-OR is correct, it does not provide an engineering path. We cannot currently design or control quantum coherence in microtubules. We cannot build artificial systems that implement Orch-OR dynamics. The theory, even if true, offers no guidance for the candidate architecture of Chapter 17. The classical spiking approach, by contrast, is implementable on existing neuromorphic hardware today.

E.5 What Quantum Approaches Contribute to the Book's Argument

Setting Orch-OR aside as an engineering path does not mean dismissing the philosophical insight it embodies. Penrose's deepest contribution is not the microtubule proposal — it is the Gödelian argument that genuine mathematical understanding may be non-algorithmic. If this argument is sound, it implies that no computational architecture, however complex and however well it satisfies the structural requirements of Chapters 13 and 17, will produce the kind of understanding that Penrose identifies as distinctively conscious. This is structurally parallel to the Dzogchen objection of Chapter 19: both identify a boundary that engineering, operating within its classical framework, may not cross. Penrose locates the boundary in the physics of computation; Dzogchen locates it in the ontology of awareness itself. Both deserve to be taken seriously, neither dissolves by building a better spiking network, and both remain genuinely open at the close of this book.

www.ingramcontent.com/pod-product-compliance
Lightning Source LLC
LaVergne TN
LVHW090320210926
848480LV00001B/304